"A great and fun read for anybody who has a boss. It incorporates pragmatic approaches and best practices to help lesson friction and therefore stress-whether at the workforce or home."

Mr. Wilson Cheng
Director of a major technology company in the USA

"Mind challenging and liberating. Needed for anyone in a rapidly expanding company whether you are a boss, manager or staff."

David Loke, Readyspace CEO

"Having a great relationship with your boss is critical to your happiness and your success at work. With his extensive management consulting experience, Low offers practical hand-on insights and advices on working well with your boss. By following his integrated framework is the smart way to avoid the process of trial and error."

Dr. William Chen, General Manager (HK), Royal Dynasty International Holdings; Adjunct Professor, Griffith University

"It is an excellent book about working "hand-in-hand" with your boss creating tangible value for your employer contributing to your successful career development!"

Dr. Gerry Li, Adjunct Associate Professor,
Hong Kong University of Science and Management
Consultant on Design Thinking,
Business Model, KPIs and OKRs.

How to T.O.R.T.U.R.E. Your Boss

A Practical Result-Oriented Approach to Working Well with Your Boss

Jimmy Low

PARTRIDGE

Copyright © 2019 by Jimmy Low.

ISBN: Hardcover   978-1-5437-4933-5
       Softcover   978-1-5437-4931-1
       eBook   978-1-5437-4932-8

All rights reserved. No part of this book may be used or reproduced by any means, graphic, electronic, or mechanical, including photocopying, recording, taping or by any information storage retrieval system without the written permission of the author except in the case of brief quotations embodied in critical articles and reviews.

Because of the dynamic nature of the Internet, any web addresses or links contained in this book may have changed since publication and may no longer be valid. The views expressed in this work are solely those of the author and do not necessarily reflect the views of the publisher, and the publisher hereby disclaims any responsibility for them.

Print information available on the last page.

To order additional copies of this book, contact
Toll Free 800 101 2657 (Singapore)
Toll Free 1 800 81 7340 (Malaysia)
orders.singapore@partridgepublishing.com

www.partridgepublishing.com/singapore

CONTENTS

INTRODUCTION 1
- Do you really have a boss? 1
- When is your immediate superior a boss? 5

LEVEL 1 9
- The Seven Strategic Rules For Reducing
  Boss-Subordinate Tension 9
- Re-charging Your Emotional Battery 10
- An Overview of the Seven Tension-Reducing Rules 11
- Rule 1 12
- Rule 2 17
- Rule 3 22
- Rule 4 27
- Rule 5 32
- Rule 6 37
- Rule 7 41

LEVEL 2 47
- The Seven Tactical Steps In Managing A
  Turnaround Strategy 47
- Increasing Your Intellectual Power 48
- Optimizing: The Only Chance to Keep Your
  Boss at Bay 49
- An Overview of the 7-Step Approach 51
- Step #1: Target-Setting 53
- Step #2: Observing 59
- Step #3: Recording 67
- Step #4: Tracking 75
- Step #5: Unravelling 81
- Step #6: Re-defining 94
- Step #7: Expediting 101

CONCLUSION **107**
- Are you yourself a BOSS?..107
- Taking Stock Of What You Have Achieved......................108
- Self-Perception Check Quiz 110
- Verdict: Are You A First Among Equals........................... 111

INTRODUCTION

T.O.R.T.U.R.E.

DO YOU REALLY HAVE A BOSS?

Any person who is a Snobbishly-Obsessive Bully is bad enough. To find in the same person a Sneaky Snobbishly-Obsessive Bully (i.e., S.S.O.B. or read as Double S.O.B.) is certainly a double misfortune for anyone who has to deal with this beast (aptly nicknamed as the Double S.O.B.) most of one's waking moments.

And when you discover that the Double S.O.B. when spelt in reverse is actually your own boss, what a catastrophe! You want to pack up and go immediately, but can you?

Throughout the book, gender-specific terms may be used in order to ease the text flow. Whenever a gender-specific term is used, it should be understood as referring to both genders, unless explicitly stated. This is done solely for the purpose of making the text easier to read, and no offense or sexism is intended.

Your boss is all right as a person whom you hardly know.

Once you know him not as another person, colleague, acquaintance, or friend, but as a boss, he does not exist as a person any more. He becomes a monster. You begin to loathe him. That is because he is not what he appears to be to the public at large.

You'll discover that a friend is seldom ever a good boss, but a boss who does not claim to be one or who does not behave like one is always your friend.

Your immediate superior is to you either a boss or one who is First Among Equals.

The reality is that the person to whom you report immediately is caught in the dichotomy of hypocrisy and authenticity in management.

Hypocrisy in management, at one extreme, produces the character nicknamed the Double S.O.B. Authenticity in management, at the other extreme, produces leaders nicknamed the First Among Equals.

Is your immediate superior a Boss or a First Among Equals?

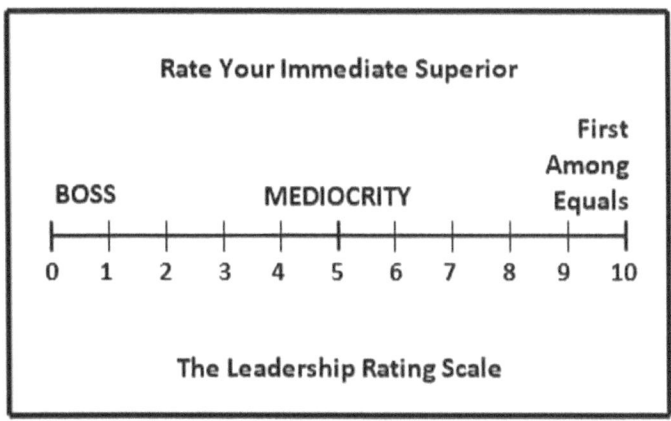

The boss makes your life in the organization worth leaving, the sooner the better.

The boss is out to give you a real rough time, the rougher the better.

The boss is desperate in driving home to you that he is the boss. He makes all the decisions, the more the merrier.

The boss's battle is won when your self-confidence is shattered, when you can't do anything without him or without his prior knowledge and consent.

If your immediate superior respects and treats you as an equal, he makes your life in the organization worth living, the longer the better.

As your immediate superior, he is First Among Equals. He leads and manages with the highest level of integrity and with a code of professional ethics.

He builds your self-esteem. He encourages you to tackle strategic issues. He learns with you. He builds in you the belief that supports you all the way.

The First Among Equals truly and progressively empowers you as you progress with confidence and competence along the fast corporate track.

WHEN IS YOUR IMMEDIATE SUPERIOR A BOSS?

WHEN HE IS A BLAME-FIXER.

When something goes wrong, his primary concern is to fix the blame. Instead of swiftly helping to mitigate the damage brought about by the unexpected consequences, he wants to know right away who is to be blamed. If he is unable to get any name from you, you will end up as the unfortunate scapegoat. "Why did you let this happen?" "What the hell have you been doing?" "Why do I need you for?" "You'd better answer for this." That's what he will typically say.

When is your immediate superior a boss?

WHEN HE IS AN ORDER-GIVER.

As an out-and-out boss-pleaser, he is a perfect yes-man to whatever whims and fancies coming from his immediate superior, who is to be expected, another boss. The result is under the pretext of delegation, he becomes a polished order-giver. Like a serf in medieval England, you go to bed each night not knowing what you will be ordered to do the next day. Herein lies the principal source of your mental stress. To make matters worse, any memo from him to you is made up of scribbled notes hardly decipherable no matter how hard you try. What is clearly decipherable is his fanatical insistence that anything sent to his boss must be PERFECT! You will be subjected to all kinds of verbal harassment should he spot an error in what you submit through him to his boss.

When is your immediate superior a boss?

WHEN HE IS STATUS-SEEKER.

As an egocentric and protocol-conscious corporate climber, his thirst to make his office symbolic of high power and prestige is unquenchable. Accessibility to his presence is restricted to those much higher up in the organizational hierarchy. Any matter from you to him is given no priority, unless it is something that affects his status-an invitation, for example, to be with important people at important public events. His eyebrows are raised should you address him by his first name. His secretary is untouchable as she exists to serve only him. If you ever find your 5-feet-?-inches stature in his room, you will not be permitted to leave till you are reduced to an inch tall!

When is your immediate superior a boss?

WHEN HE IS A SQUELER.

The picture he paints of you before his colleagues is that of a pain in the neck. Indeed, he does not have a kind word for you at all. Privately he has been feeding back to his immediate superior nasty and unfair things about you. That you are abdicating your role as a supervisor. That you are not sharing key information with the others. That you need to go for training in goal-setting and motivation. Perhaps his conscience is pricking him. He wants to project his role as one that is indispensable to the organization. He wants the world to know that he is getting people very much below the ordinary to produce results.

The BOSS	**The First Among Equals**
• Creates work to justify each payroll dollar. • Goes for the form first and last and never the substance. • Treats things as people and people as things. • Hopes that by doing things right they become the right things to do. • Uses cost as the first and final decisive factor. • Prefers you to say. "Tell me what to do."	• Creates value for each customer dollar spent. • Goes for the substance first and then the form. • Treats people as people and things as things. • Hankers after doing the right things followed by doing things right. • Uses ROI (return on investment) as a decisive factor. • Prefers you to say. "I suggest this is what we should do."

If you do have a boss what's the worst thing that can possibly happen to you?

You will not lose your life. You will lose only your job. And it will be a lousy, stressful, thankless job that you will be losing when you have over you the Double S.O.B.

So cheer up inside you although you have ceased to smile from your heart ever since the reign of terror began.

You don't need to quit your job as yet, but you need to quit thinking of quitting.

If you follow the rules in Part I and the steps in Part II as spelt out in the acronym T.O.R.T.U.R.E. you will be able to manage a turnaround strategy, effectively and successfully.

So, let's see how you can begin to T.O.R.T.U.R.E. your boss!

LEVEL 1

T.O.R.T.U.R.E.

THE SEVEN STRATEGIC RULES FOR REDUCING BOSS-SUBORDINATE TENSION

RE-CHARGING YOUR EMOTIONAL BATTERY

At level 1, the strategic rules emerging from the acronym T.O.R.T.U.R.E. form the basis for the building of a self-awareness system. The system allows you to strengthen your self-defence mechanism so that it can better withstand the constant bombardment from your boss against your self-confidence and self-esteem.

You need to work with better focus and concentration on your job. Despite working with gloom and terror hanging over your head, you can still be productive, creative, and enduring. To achieve that, the system provides psychological relief as summed up by the acronym:

> **T** hrough
> **O** n-going
> **R** ationalization,
> **T** o
> **U** nlock
> **R** elief
> **E** motionally.

AN OVERVIEW OF THE SEVEN TENSION-REDUCING RULES

Rule #1: Provides a way out of office gossip and politics and out of any possible verbal arguments with your boss.

Rule #2: Reduces the risk of getting a reprimand from your boss when you undertake work that is non-routine and non-repetitive.

Rule #3: Calls attention to what it involves to be able to emerge from the ashes of disenchantment as a promising and rising employee on the corporate fast track.

Rule #4: Sets out the proper decorum that marks you as a person capable of detecting and defusing mines that may be planted all over your department or organization.

Rule #5: Inculcates in you the action-oriented habit and practice that will get things moving and make ideas happen quickly before your boss calls you up.

Rule #6: Shows how the ambience of your office can be re-adjusted to match and reflect the high professional status to which you should rise despite the current misery you are experiencing.

Rule #7: Elevates your vision to a higher career horizon and protects you from any psychological intimidation from your boss.

RULE 1

Talk back, never; nor talk behind your boss' back. But if you do talk, talk only when talked to, and talk laconically or in monosyllables.

Anything you want to say to another person about this beast who is a living terror to your life in the organization is a taboo.

The least said, inside or outside the organization, the least you want to say, the least you want to think about it, the soonest it is mended.

You are not able to remove the beast or tame the beast by telling others about him or about your agonies and your anxieties. The worst thing is that what you say will be fed back a hundredfold to the beast through the grapevine and you will begin to live in the reign of aggravated terror. It will be for you out of the frying pan into the fire! As the proverbial saying goes, two wrongs do not make a right.

In your division, department or section where the head is a boss, the climate will be such that trust, harmony and co-operation will never be fostered and nurtured among your colleagues.

Rivalry, bad-mouthing and back-stabbing will be the order of each working day. Everyone will try to get some breathing space by getting someone else's name into the Boss' Black Book. In the reign of terror, everyone is a potential traitor or blackmailer. So, trust no one and keep your mouth shut. Walls have ears.

No doubt you are disgusted by the beastly behavior of your boss. But do you deserve to be bottled up the whole day or worst still after work?

You should say to yourself that no one including this beast can cause you to lose your cool and temper and to be bottled up without your consent.

You need to reassure yourself that you are what you think you are. What your boss thinks you are or what beastly things he says about you will not make an iota of difference from what you truly are.

You should begin to focus more intensely on your work, your career, your family, your hobbies and your future. Take the next bold step to dream of the impossible dream— to visualize what you want to accomplish in life, what you intend to do three years down the road. Fill your mind with ideas and all kinds of possibilities that you may one day end up with. There is no room in your mind for any thoughts about this beastly superior of yours. There are far more important and worthwhile things in life to get you mentally engaged in than the Double S.O.B.!

You should not take the bait or fall into the trap where whatever you say can be conveniently and deceptively twisted and distorted and promptly communicated to your boss, and right away, like a sly fox waiting for its prey, he will pounce on you. A good rule of thumb is therefore: see no evil, hear no evil, think no evil and speak no evil.

Beastly he has become. Of his mental stability it will be up to the psychiatrist to say. Of his style of management reflecting his deep-rooted personality, it will be up to the psychologist to say. As you have not worked with him nor has he worked with you, it is not for you to say what sort of worker he is. As you are simply working under him, you will learn to take orders and conform to them, and there is nothing else to comment about. Let anyone who asks what you think of him to find it out for himself, and to draw his own conclusion. For yourself, the boss as a subject of talk or thought is always a taboo. Period.

Nor are you obliged in any way to talk or speak or think kindly of him. That would amount to hypocrisy or false modesty. As far as you are concerned you have already psychologically conditioned your mind while at work as well as after work to be far removed from any thought of the beast.

This is not to say that you ought to recognize that an interpersonal conflict exists between you and him, and that you have decided to throw in the towel and have decided not to think about it.

Ironically, there is no conflict at all, and even if there is, it is not interpersonal, because there are no personal reasons that might have brought both of you together.

If ever there is any reason why you and he have come together, it must be an organizational reason, and not a personal, reason, having known what a beast he is! So, if there is any conflict, it would be an intra-organizational conflict. No wonder no interpersonal skills training course has been able to help you to tame or turn this beast around.

The fact of the situation is that it is not in the true sense an organizational reason that has actually brought both of you together. Either he has simply been appointed to be your immediate superior or you have merely been instructed to report to him. There is no pre-matching of the compatibility between you and him so far as the chemistry goes, or a pre-matching of the different areas of expertise and experience that would produce the synergy that would be required for the accomplishment of some strategic goal, or a prior discussion and agreement on what would be expected of and from you and him.

If after all this has been done, and both he and you cannot see eye to eye on some professional aspects of the work, an intra-organizational conflict may exist. Both can then begin to negotiate. But with an immediate superior who is a boss, it is not an intra-organizational conflict in which you are caught; it is a Double S.O.B. that you are facing.

So there is no kind word or an unkind word for him coming from you. Nor will you be drawn into any dialogue, conversation or controversy, inside or outside the organization when his name is mentioned or when it is possible that the person referred to is your boss.

Even when it is legitimate for you to open your mouth, don't open it too wide or for too long. This may be at meetings with him in his office or with others whether or not the beast is present or around.

His attention span for you is only three seconds, whereas he can appear to be very attentive for hours on end when his boss talks. So what's the point wasting your breath? Be laconic. Use monosyllables.

In contrast, his questions for you are badly punctuated and hardly intelligible and without focus. Each question is meant to reveal your vulnerabilities. In eight out of ten cases, a simple "Yes." answer will suffice. For example, "How come when others can do it for 'x' dollars and taking only 'y' months to complete, you need a bigger budget and a longer time frame, and notwithstanding that you have been given better and bigger machines, so your disparity is still subject to some analysis and to be substantiated by some figures, I suppose, you have not worked on them yet?" With such a multi-faceted, fault-finding question, the best you can do in the circumstances is just say, "Yes."

Most of the time when you simply could not figure out what beastly things he is trying to ask or say, then simply turn your "Yes" answer into a rhetoric question, "Yes?". He may resort angrily, "Yes, what?" Your response will still be a calm "Yes?" If he still barks back, "To what, your yes?" Your response will then be, "Yes, sir!" If you are driven to your wit's end, you may then say, "Yes. Yes?"

RULE 2

O btain a go from him before you set a goal, or make a go for anything new.

The boss wants to know everything, rumours and gossips included. From you he wants to know what is happening on the ground and in the air, and what you are up to. Acquiring this knowledge from you without putting it to practical use is an exercise in futility. How you wish the Double S.O.B. could use the knowledge……..

- to advise you on how to navigate across uncharted waters

- to help you plan in advance

- to agree with you on re-structuring existing work

- to review with you budgetary limits and controls, and to re-allocate resources strategically

- to agree with you on a contingency plan

He gets extremely annoyed if his boss happens to ask him about some new things happening in the organization and you have not either consulted him first or at least kept him informed. He will come down hard on you. So before you do anything new, don't proceed yet. Always remember:

Act in haste, repent at leisure.

Often you may experience the utter awkwardness you are in when at a meeting your boss suddenly throws at you a question which finds you dumbfounded.

The trouble with this beast of yours is his inability to ask the right question at the right time. So, you are caught without the right answer for the wrong question! No fault of yours, clearly.

A manager is paid to think and to make decisions. As a prime decision-making tool, asking the right question at the right time is invaluable to any manager. Without this tool, a manager will never emerge as a true leader. He may be a loafer (like the average person in the final year of his retirement), or a looter (like a common thief pilfering from everywhere) or like your boss, a lunatic (see the diagram below).

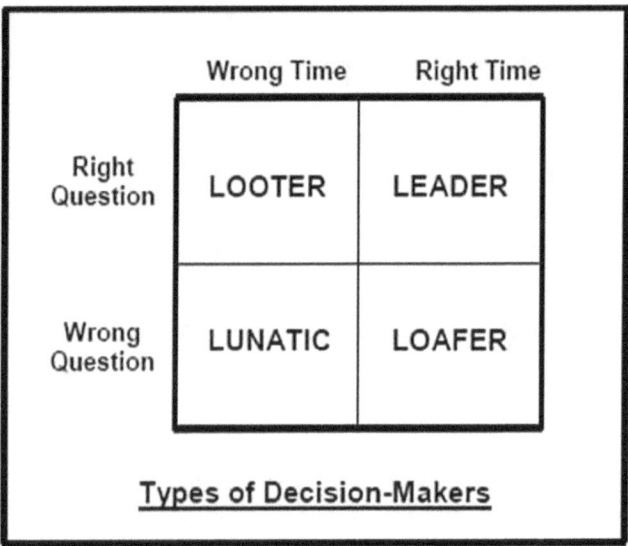

Between thirty-five and fifty-five percent of your prime time may be spent in trying to find and provide him with the information he wants, not necessarily the information he actually needs.

You can reduce the stress you have as a result of having to manage from one crisis to another by setting up a more efficient, responsive and comprehensive system of collecting, keeping and retrieving information, either manually or with the aid of a pc.

If you know what you need to update this unpredictable beast, you will know what and when to collect, keep and transmit and how to go about collecting, keeping and transmitting the needed information.

There will be less hassle if you are not responsible for the work of others, such as when you have subordinates reporting directly to you.

You need to let him know what you are doing, from whom you receive work, and to whom you pass your finished or semi-finished work.

The frequency with which your Double S.O.B. asks with urgency for information from you is frightful. To reduce this frequency there are seven aspects of your work about which information should be periodically fed back to him. They are:

- How is your performance technically and objectively measured?

- What is the activity level of your work in terms of the number of hours you have to put in for any specific task or group of tasks?

- How is your output calculated or quantified?

- What are your targets: daily, weekly, and monthly?

- What are your achievements?

- If there is a shortfall, what are the reasons, and how do you intend to recoup the difference?

- Are you facing work-related problems and what do you intend to do about them?

The Double S.O.B. may not ask any of these important questions. Nevertheless, you will have to answer them, and pass the information to him, the sooner the better.

If you are carrying out a project, let your boss have a one-page memo with concise and succinct answers to the following nine questions.......

- What is the project aimed at achieving?

- Who has instructed or requested that the project be done and when has clearance to proceed with the project been given?

- What is the primary problem the project intends to resolve?

- What is the estimated cost of the project or the part in which you are involved?

- When will the project be completed?

- With whom are you working?

- What are the intermediate goals?

- How frequent do you intend to keep your boss posted of the status and progress of the project?

- How many man-hours must you put in on a daily and weekly basis?

If you have subordinates reporting to you, let the Double S.O.B. have a one-page weekly-rolling memo with answers to the following eight questions....

- Why does the section (or department) exist?

- If the work of the section (or department) stops, how will the organization or any part of the organization be affected?

- What are the targets that have to be achieved: daily, weekly and monthly?

- Who is doing what in your section (or department)?

- How is the performance of each employee measured?

- What special events or functions will be held next week, next month?

- Who will be involved in each of the special functions and what will each of those involved be doing specifically?

- In what appropriate way should your boss be involved in each of the special events or functions?

RULE 3

Revitalize your current knowledge of your job as well as your current knowledge of the company's product and service *vis-à-vis* your competitor's product and service.

A manager is as good as his knowledge of his job as well as his knowledge of the product or service his company sells.

Job knowledge refers to the technical way a product or service is designed and developed, or out-sourced, modified or customized, priced, packaged, promoted and delivered with post-sales service. It deals with two major areas of the manager's work: the job content and the job context.

Product knowledge refers to the level of understanding and appreciation of the technical features, functions and benefits of the company's product as well as an understanding and appreciation of the differences that exist between the company's product or service and those of the company's major competitors.

To expect your Double S.O.B. to be rated high on both dimensions in terms of his job knowledge and product knowledge is to expect a leopard to change its spots overnight. Your immediate superior would be the First Among Equals had he been highly knowledgeable about his job as a whole and about his company's product *vis-à-vis* his competitor's product. The First Among Equals is a builder, who guides and instructs with a vision, supported by a high technical competence (see the diagram below).

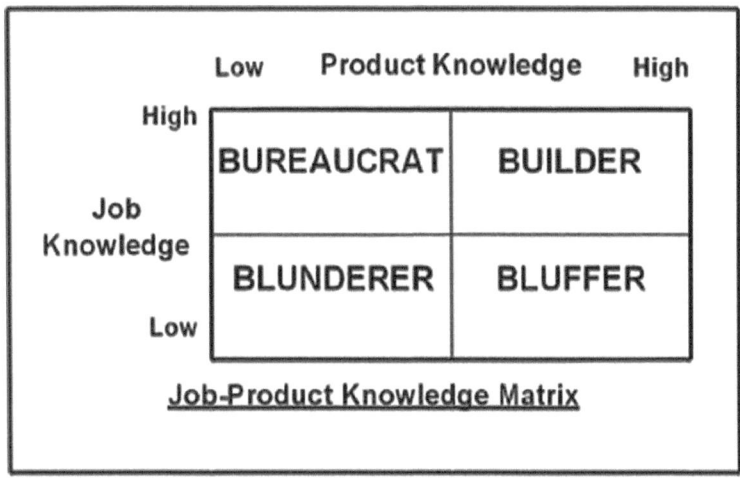

Job-Product Knowledge Matrix

Your Double S.O.B. will tend to be a blunderer, who with a garrison mentality runs, but does not manage the department or section; or a bureaucrat, who places barbed wires around your work; or a bluffer, who promises his boss and clients things which he actually hopes they will soon forget.

Emerging from the job-product knowledge matrix, there are three major styles with which your boss may approach work, while the First Among Equals has only one work orientation style as the diagram below shows.

	Product Knowledge	
	Low	High
Job Knowledge High	Ready. Fire! Aim.	Ready. Aim. Fire!
Job Knowledge Low	Fire! Fire! Fire!	Fire! Aim. Ready.

Four Work Orientation Styles

The "Ready, Fire, Aim." mentality tends never to get new things off the ground. Getting things perfectly analyzed, getting things perfectly organized and getting all plans perfectly documented, all these become the major focus of your boss' job.

The "Fire, Fire, Fire." mentality gets everybody including suppliers and external contractors busy really for nothing. "The more we do, the more blame we get!" is the feeling of everybody at the shop floor or at the frontline. Your boss' job is to impress on his boss how busy the department or section is!

The "Fire, Aim, Ready." mentality gets people moving in a new direction without taking stock of the resources, the expertise and the technology which exist and which are required. Your boss' job is first of all, to sell; secondly, to sell even if you don't have it; and lastly, to sell even if you don't know where to get it!

When your Double S.O.B. is averse to the one and only right style in approaching work, that is, "Ready, Aim, Fire!" you will be recovering from crisis to crisis!

The only person on whom you can rely to get the right job done right is yourself. If you can by incremental degree acquire every day a new level of product knowledge as well as job knowledge, no matter how little the new knowledge may be, in a year's time, you would have acquired an immense amount of practical knowledge to make you an expert in a particular field.

You should lay hands on at least one good book that extends the frontiers of your knowledge about your job every month. You may also wish to place for a trial period a year's subscription on your own expense for an excellent journal to increase your product knowledge.

When you continuously increase both your job knowledge and product knowledge you'll not only alleviate the stress you get from the Double S.O.B. but also increase the marketability of your professional knowledge and expertise in your chosen career.

A great boost to your own creativity will be if you can read outside your particular discipline or subject area. There are now in many book stores books on specialized subjects written by specialists for non-specialists. You should always be on the look-out for books such as those listed below:

- Finance for Non-Financial Managers
- Finance for Human Resources Managers
- Finance for Marketing Managers
- Marketing for Non-Marketing Managers
- Business Law for Non-Legal Practitioners

- Production Management for Marketing Managers

- Marketing for Production Managers

- Marketing for Financial Managers

- Human Capital Management for Non-Personnel Managers

- Contract Law for Purchasing Managers

To recapitulate:

> You must take ownership of the responsibility to grow in your own career and to make every effort to progress along the career path you've chosen. More so, when you have a Double S.O.B. over you, your career development, as well as your career advancement, lies in you own hands.

RULE 4

Toe the line, but be on your toes as you are in the enemy's mine field.

When the General orders, "Attack the hill before you. Now!" there is no hesitation among the soldiers to do as ordered at once. There is no thought of questioning, "Why this hill? Why not the next hill?" There is no "Yes, but." response.

In the organization, orders and instructions are similarly to be clearly understood and executed immediately and without question, whether you agree with them or not. Also whether they come directly from the Chief Executive Officer or from the Double S.O.B.

There is only one question that you always need to ask. And that is whether or not the instruction or task to be carried out is understood by you as what the Double S.O.B. has intended to mean. If in doubt, promptly write out what you think he has meant on a memo pad and send it to him through his secretary for quick confirmation.

One stereotyped instruction fondly used by many a Double S.O.B. is "Please handle", an order which is scribbled at the top of a memo or a letter.

If the memo or the letter is one which you have actually handled before, then the task before you is a repetitive and routine one. You can proceed with haste to accomplish it.

If the memo or the letter calls for the execution of a non-routine task or a task which is new to you or which is not done before, you should outline what you intend to do in the margin if space allows, otherwise in another note to be attached to the memo or letter. End your outline with something to this effect: "If you agree, I'll proceed as outlined."

The following flow chart may be of some help to you:

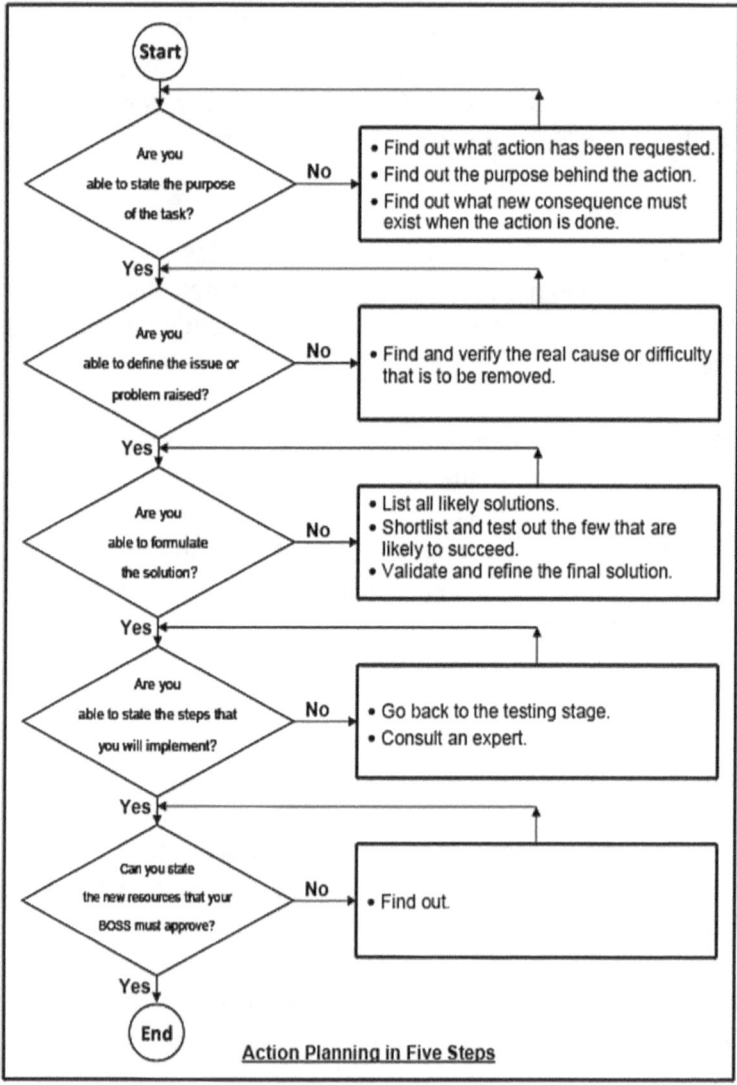

Action Planning in Five Steps

In your analysis of what you think you should do, you need to determine upfront who else outside your department or section may be required to help you with the task. You need to let your boss know and clear with him first before you approach the person or the person's immediate supervisor for assistance.

You also need to determine upfront what new or additional resources are required, where they can be obtained and at what cost. You need to surface your requirements to your boss and get his written approval first before you proceed to acquire the resources with or without the assistance of the Purchasing Department depending on the policy of your company.

From the living terror of the organization when there is no mention about when the task is to be done, it would mean that you need to do it right away. Any delay is at your own risk. That is clearly an unwise thing to do. In fact, to cope with this your sense of urgency and anticipation must come to your rescue. You should learn to anticipate what he wants done and do it before he says so.

The Double S.O.B. will be looking for any slip you make to pounce hard on you. If you ever get any job or any task messed up you would surely have had it! If you're caught not following any office or work procedures, you will promptly receive a letter of reprimand with a copy inserted into your personal file, kept by the Staff or HR Department.

So, before you send out a memo you need to make doubly sure that:

- The person to whom the memo is sent is the rightful recipient.

- The recipient can act on what you have requested based on all the information you have sent.

- If you are not sure to whom to write you must check with the living terror. It is better to get a scolding from him before any error is actually made, than to be severely taken to task after the fact.

You need to check whether all the necessary information has been stated. For example, when you are informing addressees about a forthcoming meeting they are to attend, you would have informed them of the purpose of the meeting, the agenda items, the date and time of the meeting, who are involved and what key decisions will be made. But you may inadvertently left out the venue!

When your work involves others especially sub-contractors or even colleagues in your own section or department, you must confirm with them in writing what they have agreed to do in terms of

- The nature and scope of the work

- The completion date

- The criteria against which the work is to be measured, and

- The cost and who will bear it

And not forgetting that a carbon copy of the "agreement" must be submitted to the living terror.

Other organizational mines which you need to look out for and which you must be able to defuse once you detect them may take the following subtleties:

- Forgetting to submit claim forms with supporting documents and receipts.

- Being away on medical leave without submitting an officially-approved medical certificate.

- Accepting an external assignment without the prior written approval of the proper authority.

- Helping out another colleague in another department without the prior consent of your boss.

- Being seen having lunch with a colleague who is not on speaking terms with your boss.

- Being seen during office hours doing something that does not appear to have any link or relationship to your work.

- Being seen each time talking on the telephone, or working near a photocopy machine, or standing near the water cooler, or walking into or out of the washroom!

RULE 5

Up and about on the shop floor or at the front-line you must be, but never stay longer than twelve minutes on end in your "cubicle" as you are directly in his firing line.

There are three distinct sets of people with whom you need to maintain a continuous dialogue and relationship. They are the people who have needs and expectations which they have entrusted on you to be fulfilled. They are the people who should be in your mind most if not all the time. There is therefore no more room in your mind for any thought, positive or otherwise, about your Double S.O.B.

They are the people who are the cause and not the consequence of your work. They are the people who really make or break your work. They are the real force that drives your work, not the Double S.O.B. They are also collectively the source that provides your payroll. When these people disappear from you so is your monthly pay cheque. When your living terror disappears, your pay does not. Only your unhappiness and disenchantment.

Time spent with these people must be planned ahead as part of your on-going operational strategy. Your plan should allow 65% of your time checking, clarifying, reviewing and translating the needs and expectations of these people so that you can come up with accurate SPECIFICATIONS 100% of the time. Your plan should also allow 35% of your time cross-checking, negotiating, adjusting, and fine-tuning with these people so that you can come up with right PRODUCT or SERVICE 100% of the time.

Coming up with the right specifications that will lead to the right product or service 100% of the time would in most circumstances mean spending ninety-six percent of your time away from the office or desk. Unless of course the product or service is produced at no other place than at you work-station.

Your department or section does not exist to create and generate work around the clock. Its sole and primary purpose is to create or add value to the service or product that consumers or corporate clients are delighted to buy. But because of the increasingly stiffer competition that now exists at the marketplace, your department or section must be able to create or add value at half the time it would have normally taken under non-competitive conditions.

But because your competitors may also be able to create or add even greater value to their products or services, you also need to focus on getting your product or service out at a lower cost. And not just once, but doing it continually.

You must therefore be caught and roped into the main stream of work that typifies the organization-the authentic and legitimate work of the enterprise, that is, and not the so-called work which is non-focused and un-integrated within the strategic plan of the organization, and which is therefore not only unproductive but also counter-productive.

So from time to time, stop and ask:

"Can I honestly say that what I am now engaged in doing, whether having a conversation with another colleague or with a client or with my subordinate, or working on some work that is passed to me, is positively to turn out or to help to turn out a better product or service for the company? If not, I must stop doing what I am now doing."

Who are the people you need to see in person on a regular and non-sporadic basis all the time?

They are classified into three principal sets of people (see the diagram below).

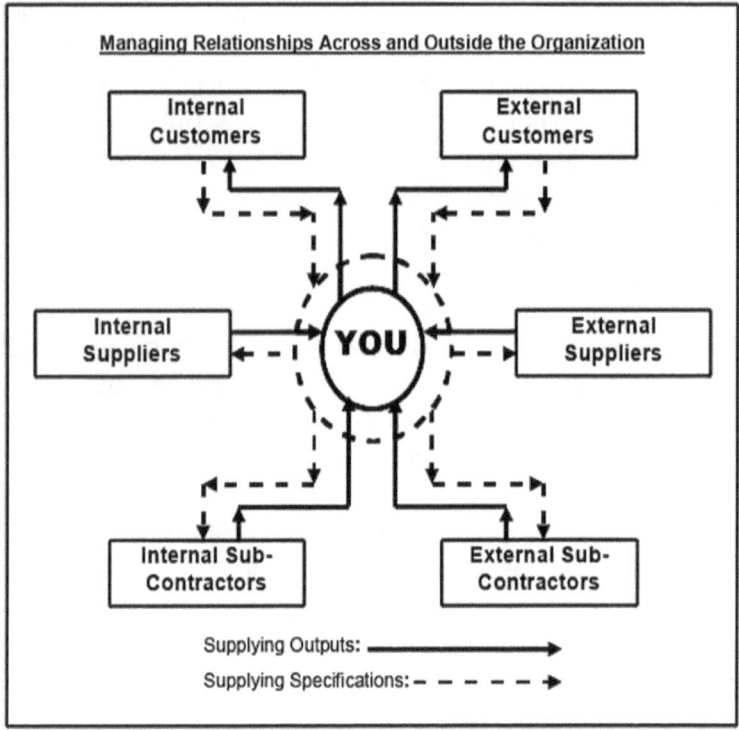

The first set of people are those who will receive your work whether in their finished or semi-finished form. They are your customers who are housed either inside or outside the organization.

The second set of people are those who either create a product for you or add value to the work you have passed to them. They are your sub-contractors who may be housed inside the organization either as your colleagues outside your department or section or as your subordinates or housed outside the organization as external sub-contractors.

The third set of people are those who will provide you with the resources: materials, machines, manpower, finance, professional advice, without which you cannot create or add value to the product or service of the company. These people are your suppliers and they can be internal as well as external.

All these people are not locked up in your room or office. They are scattered all over the organization as well as all over the country. You need to be out and about. The internet, the telephone and the fax machine have done wonders to improve and speed up communications. But their limitations, no matter how sophisticated the technology may have advanced, must be recognized and accepted. The face-to-face dialogue is still the most effective way of fostering human relationships among your contacts with the exception of your Double S.O.B., of course!

To the customers, you must supply outputs which must meet with their original specifications; to suppliers and sub-contractors, you must supply them with your specifications against which the outputs they generate must be measured.

So the key to managing or co-ordinating work with success lies in your ability to abide by this principle:

Each output or result which is the consequence of work must conform to and be compatible with its original specification, no more and no less.

If your work-station or office or room is within the direct firing-line of the living terror, the more reason why you should not be in your office. Physically, there are a couple of things you may want to try out.

First of all, re-arrange your desk so that the living terror cannot visibly see you or at the best he can see only your back. The important thing is not actually whether he can see you. It is whether you can avoid seeing him!

Secondly, are you able to get hold of some large wall calendars or posters that you can discreetly hang over the glass panel of your partition so as to block off the vision and the sight of the living terror?

Thirdly, can you arrange for a cabinet or a pc monitor or a large flowerpot with a tall plant to be placed between where the living terror sits and where you sit so that the vision from the terror can be effectively deflected?

If you can do all the three things you would be able achieve a greater peace of mind. It's all a question of whether you can get the Double S.O.B. out of your sight so as to stay out of your mind effectively.

At any rate, with so many visits you have to make to stay in touch with your customers, suppliers and sub-contractors, you should not have the "luxury" of finding yourself in your office or "cubicle" as your boss likes to call it with cynicism, each time longer than twelve minutes. In effect, you will be in and out of your office very frequently. In this way, you can reduce your boss' chance of catching you and pouncing on you whenever he has had it from his boss.

RULE 6

Remove any personal chattels such as plaques, photographs, books, journals or files from the office; better still, do without your desk or table.

One big mistake when moving into a new job is to bring with you a couple of personal chattels which you treasure most and which you begin to display on your desk, in the bookshelves or against the wall. Family photographs, academic certificates, sports awards, trophies, paintings and antiques rank high in the list of ostentatious displays that dominate the landscape of your room, office or work-station.

Under normal circumstances, particularly when you like your job because you can be identified and associated with success and happiness, because central to your work is the person to whom you are accountable for results and who has your career interest and growth at heart, it is perfectly all right to have your personal belongings that you cherish to remind you of your fondest memories which you are keen to share with all around you.

But when you have a living terror to remind you of the big mistake you have made of taking up the job, how you wish you could quit the job right away especially when you are not a family man or having to play the role of a breadwinner in your family. Thus, you do not wish to be reminded that the current family commitments, financial or otherwise, have precluded you from quitting, but quit you will at the right time, of course if you want to.

You should be able to tell your mind that you are always ready to pack up and go and that the Double S.O.B. is not holding any trump card against you; nor must you give the living terror the chance to think that he has a trump card with which he can always play.

You want to be professional and to be seen and perceived by everyone including your boss that you are a professional. A professional is never tied down to a particular job or a particular employer even if the immediate superior isn't a Double S.O.B. A professional is always in demand. The labour market extends beyond the shores of your native country. You are always free to come and go. It's up to you.

And because you may be called to take up a new post at short notice there is very little time for you to pack up and vanish. That is why you are already prepared and you want the world to know that you are always prepared. The new post may mean a windfall to you in financial terms, so that it makes good economic sense even if you have to quit within twenty-four hours to assume the new post the very next day, so that it is not the Double S.O.B. who has driven you out, but that you are ready for the next important switch in your career.

Seriously, there shouldn't be any personal items, or for that matter anything, to distract you from your minute-to-minute focus and concentration on every aspect and facet of your professional job.

It is unthinkable to find an airline pilot turning the cockpit of the aircraft into a personalized room with all kinds of personal effects prominently displayed in all conspicuous places.

Nor would it be conceivable to find a surgery in a hospital full of the surgeon's personal chattels no matter how attractively displayed they are to enhance the surgeon's self-esteem!

Your own study or bedroom at home is an entirely different matter. There you can have anything you can think of to be put up for display to rekindle your most cherished memories. Your purpose of having a sweet home is to help you to have a clean surgical cut from your work so that you can really "vacation" after five every day to regain your sanity from the living terror.

So remember:

> Treat your office as an office, and your home as a home, and not treat your office as a home and your home as an office.

Treat your office as an office, and your home as a home, and not treat your office as a home and your home as an office.

One of the most stressful things that the living terror is capable of doing is abdicating his managerial role of planning, staffing, communicating, coordinating, monitoring, and evaluating under the pretext of "delegating". Whatever he cannot do or he is unwilling to do because the work is unpleasant or difficult, he will lose no time to dump it on your desk.

So, therefore consider seriously the prospect of removing your desk entirely. You can imagine the surprise the living terror will receive. He will find there is no proper receptacle for him to dump his assignment except by throwing it on the floor or into the waste-bin to which the assignment may rightfully belong.

If you find yourself having to have a desk to be able to do your work then the conference room or the meeting room elsewhere would serve your purpose. If you have a secretary, you would be encouraged in the absence of a desk, to do dictation. The secretary, like your boss, is unable to dump everything on your desk. She will have to bring in and discuss with you what she has and you can orally instruct her accordingly. Subordinates too will have no chance to dump rubbish on you.

If you cannot remove your desk, can you opt for a smaller one? You are likely to say, "No way." Understandably, that is because paradoxically the larger the desk the higher is your status in the organization. So your boss' desk is larger than yours, and his boss' desk is much larger than his. So when you don't have a desk, you don't have a status!

Anyway, with the living terror over you, who in his right mind is still concerned about status? When you are drowning you would not be thinking of straightening your tie, would you? Your Double S.O.B. would, by nature, be a high status-seeker!

RULE 7

Eye for something beyond your current job or career, and for goodness sake avoid at all costs the eye-to –eye confrontation with him.

With the Double S.O.B. watching every move you make and ready to pounce on you at the slightest mistake you make and bad-mouthing and back-stabbing you every time before his boss and the HR Director, your rating in the organization is bound to be at its lowest ever.

Chances of your being promoted or advanced in your career are very, very slim, unless the living terror is removed from the department or organization. But his boss would have to go first, because only an incompetent manager would have failed either to recognize that your Double S.O.B. is doing havoc to employee morale, or having recognized, have failed to remove your boss from the organization so that his corrosiveness like the action of a termite could be halted.

As the saying goes, "Birds of the same feather flock together", you should not be surprised that there may be quite a number of other people who are in the organization and who are like your boss. Moreover, the things which your boss does and which get you disenchanted may be the very things that you will unconsciously inherit and do them to your subordinates!

So, you must put a stop to your thinking about the things that your Double S.O.B. does or does not do. As the proverbial advice goes, "Why worry about the birds flying over your head? If you cannot stop them from flying, you can at least stop them from building nests on your head." So get on with the business at hand, and that is to do your job and do it well, as you are going to attach more instrumental value to it than ever before.

As you shift your thought from the living terror to the real objectives of your job, you will be able to increase the contribution to the success of the enterprise on a day-to-day basis. Your job becomes not an end in itself just because of the living terror around, but an important means to an important end. So you must now see beyond your current job and career.

- What new things do you plan to do and achieve in your career?

- What new opportunities can you create three months, six months or a year from today?

- Will you be ready to assume a position of higher responsibility should your MD or CEO, who is several levels above the boss of your Double S.O.B. decide to offer you a new challenge?

- Perhaps a head-hunter somewhere outside the company is looking for you? But, will you be ready to rise to the occasion?

Specific actions you should take may be selected from one or more of the following areas:

- Enrol on an evening part-time degree or post-graduate degree course which will enable you to upgrade your professional knowledge and to receive an internationally-recognized award.

- Find one evening per week to do some part-time work in a voluntary or charity organization to extend your existing network of friends and acquaintances in business.

- Enrol on an outdoor activity organized by the YMCA or your local Community Centre to maintain your physical fitness and at the same time to meet interesting and perhaps influential people outside your existing circles.

- Set up and build a personal library of your own at home to acquire and maintain a deeper knowledge of your specialized subject and a broader knowledge of other disciplines that can impact on your professional work and career.

- Explore what big organizations need and from where they have traditionally obtained their supplies, and examine whether you can come up with a specific product or service that is better and/or cheaper than what the big organizations are currently getting so that there is a market niche you can move into as an entrepreneur.

- As you focus on your job more intensely, you need to be certain not only that the job can be done on time and within budget (certainty of outcome) but also that the job can contribute significantly to an identifiable corporate goal or objective, directly or indirectly (impact of outcome).

- You should avoid falling into the mistake that your Double S.O.B. makes. He may be sure that the job can be done, but he knows that the impact of the outcome may not be high. On the other hand, he may be sure that the job is very important to the organization, but he also knows that the job may never take off!

- Another likely scenario to note is that your boss may know that the job may be unimportant and may have difficulty in taking off, yet he does nothing about it. In fact, in all the three situations, he makes no effort either to increase the impact of the outcome or to make it certain that the outcome will take place (see the diagram below).

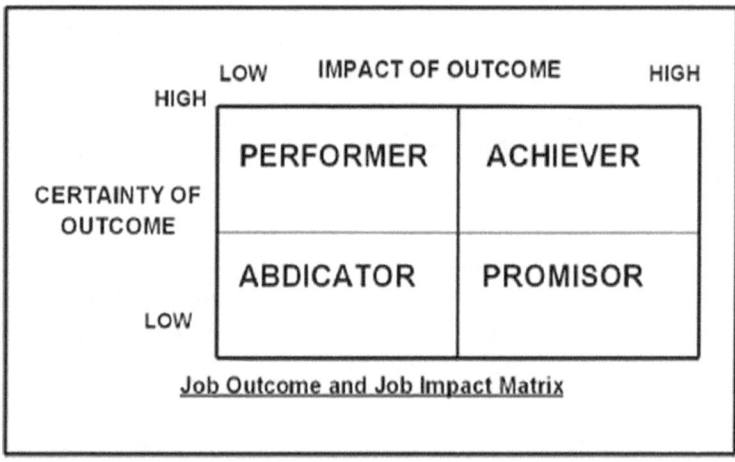

Job Outcome and Job Impact Matrix

As an achiever, you do your best to make sure that the job can be completed as planned and that the job when completed will make an important contribution to the company.

It is generally not long before your Double S.O.B. becomes an object of abomination. You would like to avoid the living terror at all costs inside and outside the organization. You should also avoid those in the organization who are part of his network that provides him with the feedback from the grapevine. The boss of the living terror should also be avoided. The less he knows or remembers you, the better.

To prevent finding yourself in the path of the living terror, know where he usually lunches and at what TIME. Use a different

Cafeteria or restaurant; otherwise go either before or after your boss.

Avoid the elevator. You are likely to bump into him or his boss. Use the stairs for climbing up and for climbing down the building. Walking allows you to think and to stay physically fit.

Be in your office before anyone arrives. Not only you will not bump into the very people you wish to avoid, you have a couple of minutes in which you can concentrate and plan ahead in absolute privacy. Leave your office on time, having ascertained that the day's work has been completed. Late hours in the office would arouse suspicion. Those who are never a fan of yours will tell the living terror all sorts of stories about your late work at the office. Besides, always leave with empty hands and come with empty hands. The living terror may instruct the security guard to check what you bring out and not so much what you bring in!

Attend meetings punctually-not a minute earlier nor a minute late. Once the meeting is over, disappear quickly. Avoid the trap of being drawn into any small talk or gossip. Keep your eyes always on the papers before you. Do sit upright and be as serious and as solemn as you can appear. Think about the objectives of the meeting; determine the specific inputs you should be contributing, the specific actions you think you should be taking if such actions fall clearly within the functions of your job.

As the source of the second firing line from the living terror is his eyes, the first firing line being his memos, the good rule of thumb is to avoid looking at him at all times.

Whether you happen to pass by him along the corridor or having to sit face to face with him at a meeting, or when replying to a question from him, you should not establish any eye contact with him.

When walking, look straight ahead of you and walk briskly.

At meetings, look at your writing pad and do some action planning or read the discussion or decision papers before you. Don't let your eyes rove around the room. They are certain to fall on the living terror.

When giving an answer, speak but with your eyes on your writing pad, otherwise look above and beyond the top of his head.

The extreme practice is to close your eyes when you talk to him or see him. This is not recommended as you may perfect the practice into such a fine art that by second nature you instantly shut your eyes when crossing the road when you think you have sighted the living terror on the other side of the road, or when talking to people dear to you!

LEVEL 2

T.O.R.T.U.R.E

THE SEVEN TACTICAL STEPS IN MANAGING A TURNAROUND STRATEGY

INCREASING YOUR INTELLECTUAL POWER

At level 2, the seven tactical steps emerging from the acronym T.O.R.T.U.R.E. provide a framework for structuring and implementing work. The steps make up an integrated approach which replaces the process of trial and error under which most people have got their fingers burnt as well as resulting in getting more bombardment from the living terror.

In order to help you approach work with the right methodology and to be able to zero in on creating certainty of achievement and creating a high impact from your work, so that your boss has no cause for complaint, the approach effectively brings out two fundamental concepts:

CONCEPT I	CONCEPT II
T argetting	**T** ackling
O bjectives	**O** bstacles
R ealistically	**R** elentlessly
T urns	**T** erminates
U p	**U** nrewarding
R esults	**R** e- work
E xpeditiously.	**E** ffectively.

OPTIMIZING: THE ONLY CHANCE TO KEEP YOUR BOSS AT BAY

Three chances out of four will find your boss coming after you and giving you a real rough time. On the other hand, you have only a twenty-five percent chance, or one out of four chances, to keep the boss away from you. Hence, you need to take full advantage of that chance, and make it happen!

Before you begin any work you must think through two major areas of your work. While you are doing your work you also need to pay attention to these two areas (see the diagram below).

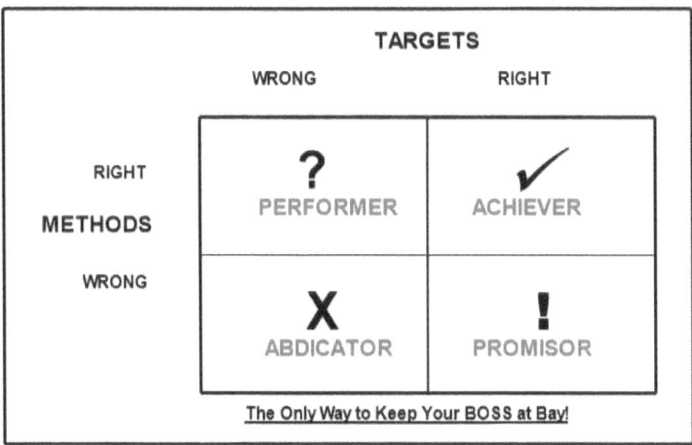

The first area is concerned with the primary purpose or ultimate function of your work. The completion of the work itself is not the primary purpose of the work. What is the work targeted at?

There is no point getting work done for the wrong objective or purpose.

The second area is concerned with whether the work is done or executed correctly. There is no point setting the right target or having the right objective, but it cannot be achieved because the work cannot be done or is done wrongly.

AN OVERVIEW OF THE 7-STEP APPROACH

Step #1: **T**arget-setting

> It defines the product of the product, the impact of the outcome or consequence of your work.

Step #2: **O**bserving

> It allows you to do an environmental scanning as part of the empirical survey or research required in order to know what the present situation is and how it can be designed or re-designed.

Step #3: **R**ecording

> It compels you to capture relevant data for factual analysis, fact control and visual impact as part of the continuous effort to improve efficiency by locating and removing wastage and defects.

Step #4: **T**racking

> It monitors, verifies, and validates each stage of the work as it progresses requiring self-assessment, self-coordination, and self-direction.

Step #5: **U**nravelling

> It directs your attention to what has gone wrong, when it has gone wrong and how to verify and remove effectively the real cause of the problem.

Step #6: **R**e-defining

> It requires you to re-examine the way you perceive, interpret, and define a work-related issue or phenomenon so that your definition is not so restrictive as to preclude the search for the right solution.

Step #7: **E**xpediting

> It opens up the whole process of each cycle of work and examines critically how the process or production time can be saved so that the total cycle time may be halved in the next round of work.

STEP #1: TARGET-SETTING

"Do I really know what should come out of an activity?"

An activity is just an activity. So in any kind of work or event or function, completing an activity itself may not be good enough. So is bringing to pass an event or a function.

In the organization there is always a purpose or an objective behind an activity. We call the real purpose behind any piece of work the target. Can you match below each activity and its target correctly by linking each numeral with an appropriate letter?

Activity Target

1	Answering an enquiry	A	Making customers want to return
2	Drafting a sales letter	B	Drawing in the crowds
3	Fixing nuts on wheels	C	Maintaining tidiness unnoticeably
4	Selling cosmetics	D	Proving what it can do uniquely
5	Doing 200 pushups	E	Creating a new customer
6	Replacing window displays	F	Increasing consumption of food
7	Receiving payments	G	Creating new orders
8	Serving drinks	H	Providing trouble-free driving
9	Demonstrating a product	I	Acquiring physical endurance
10	Sweeping the floors	J	Creating more beauty-conscious users

Activities keep us busy. Activities keep us running all over the place. Activities exhaust our energy and concentration. Activities eat up company's time. Activities drain up company's resources. Activities must therefore be accurately and precisely targeted.

2.5	4.1	6.8	8.F	10.C
1.E	3.H	5.I	7.A	9.D

Answers

We all know that as motorists before we set forth on a journey we don't choose the road first. We decide where we want to go. The destination becomes our target. We then decide which road we should take. The choice of a particular road may depend on a number of other factors. But whichever road we choose it must help us reach our final destination.

But when we approach work in the organization we seldom ask what the "destination" of our work is. Where are we heading? Are we sure we can hit our target by the work we have chosen to do?

As an example, the activity before you is to draft a sales letter, which in our analogy, is the "road" you have chosen. Now you must work mentally in reverse. You need to ask what the target is which the letter is to hit. If to increase sales is the target, the next thing you need to do is to define your target accurate enough so that you can tell when you have hit it. If the objective or purpose of any activity is vague or broad, it cannot tell when you have arrived at your "destination".

Supposing, the target of your sales latter is to increase sales by thirty percent in the next three months. Now you must ask whether the sales letter can do the job as intended. Will the people who read the sales letter pick up the telephone and start to place their orders? Or will they return the order forms? If most people don't even bother to read the sales letter, your target is beyond achievement. Your effort would have been wasted. Perhaps have you set your target too high?

A target should be expressed in as few words as possible. It must be relevant to the work of the department or the relevant to the business plan or strategy of the organization.

You may need to lower your original target. Instead, you may want to target your sales letter towards getting people to visit your retail outlet. The question you need to answer now will be, "How can I draft the letter in such a way that it will make anyone who reads the letter want to visit the shop?" You may not be able to hit the bull's eye with a hundred percent achievement. You may have to content with a fifty percent score, meaning that for every two persons who read, only one feels inclined to accept your invitation.

BOSSES assign work and leave one to figure out what its target is. At times your Double S.O.B. may even use the word "target", but in its broad sense, as the goal to be achieved remains vague and undefined.

Leaders, on the other hand, always set targets and specify what they are. Having explained and clarified what the targets are, leaders will invite you to suggest what "roads" to take. They may contribute ideas in an encouraging and creative way. They will then leave you to do the work, undisturbed. But they will make themselves available, if necessary, for consultation.

Your Double S.O.B. will say, "Quick, draft me a sales letter. On your Double! " A leader will say, "We intend to increase our sales of x product by 30% over the next twelve weeks. What methods should we use?"

It is far more productive to work with a target that has been clearly spelt out first. It is much less productive to work within the four walls of a given activity without knowing precisely what the target is.

Once it is clear what the target is, there are different ways of achieving the target. One way may cost more money; another way may need more time; another way may involve more people; and another way may require a new technology. Yet, the extent of success of each way may vary according to how success is defined.

To recapitulate: an activity leads to a result or a consequence; it is a means rather than an end. A target is the new state of affairs brought about by an event or an activity; it is the final outcome or result that provides a more durable effect on the department or the organization.

So, before you swing into action on a piece of work, you should always ask, "Towards what is this activity targeted?" Also, before you start the activity you must be able to answer the question: "Will I be able to tell when I have hit the target?"

> **T** argets
> **O** ff-course,
> **R** ejects
> **T** rebled;
> **U** tter
> **R** emorse
> **E** nsues.

Target-setting, as the first step in keeping your boss at arm's length, requires you to know precisely and concisely what the primary purpose of each activity or task is. If the activity has been assigned without a target, you need to work in reverse by figuring out what the impact or the outcome ought to be. If in doubt, you need to write out the target and check it with your boss.

A target must be realistic enough and be attainable to make the doing of the activity meaningful and motivating.

A target must be measurable, e.g. "To get one out of two recipients of the letter turning up at the main store."

A target may be expressed in qualitative terms with indicators attached, e.g., "Enhancing the value of each purchase with the purchaser walking away smiling, cheerful and full of appreciative remarks about the value he has got from what he has paid."

A target may be time-specific, e.g., "To sell the existing stock of product X in two weeks' time, starting from June 15th."

Setting the right target or understanding what the target really means as set by another person becomes a vital step in any work process.

Swing into the habit now of always starting work with the right question, "What is the target?"

By way of practice, if you are answering telephone enquiries what might be the target of your work?

Giving the right information to each enquirer? That is not the target. That is precisely what you do. That is an activity, not a target. An activity is often triggered by something external to the doer. If the enquirer did not call, you would not be giving him or her the right information, would you?

To achieve a target you need to initiate an action of your own. It may be doing something other than giving out correct information.

For example the target may be to create a new customer. This would mean that when a person calls to ask for information you instantly recognize this as an opportunity to create a new customer.

You will also look at other opportunities to create new customers such as asking existing customers for leads to enable you to contact prospective customers, or arranging office or home visits to make sales presentations.

So, if answering telephone enquiries is to create new customers, what you do must be more than simply giving out the right information. You need to put into motion the right selling process which recognizes all callers as prospective customers and which therefore turns all enquiries into triggers leading to sales being made as your prime goal.

So, remember:

> "Work is not the cause of our existence in the organization; targets are, if they are specific, relevant, realizable, meaningful, measurable, and time-bound."

STEP #2: OBSERVING

"Do I know what really needs doing and how to get started?"

If there is one reason why we are blessed with two eyes but with only one mouth, it is that we need to see twice as much as we talk, and spend twice as much time in the process.

Step two of our strategy to keep the living terror at bay is using our eyes to observe. Observing is different from seeing. Observing is looking at things intently and with a purpose. Seeing is merely allowing our eyes to wander and pick up whatever strikes the eyes.

What can be achieved by observing?

- It allows you to touch base with reality, knowing what is actually happening.

- It enables you to measure the gap between "What is" (a fact) and "What should be" (a standard or an expectation).

- It triggers new ideas and thoughts in a creative way when you start to reflect on what you have discovered.

- It facilitates the reasoning process by which you can prove a rule or principle by what you have collected, or by which you can establish a rule or principle to explain a given phenomenon which has been constantly observed.

- It allows you to link what you intend to do with what you have done so that continuity can be effectively maintained.

Very often work is left undone: an idea remains as an idea; a project exists only in print; minutes of meetings run into hours of inaction; follow-up work lapses, so is the memory of the assignor. Delay and deferment then set in. Suddenly, like a thunder in the sky, your Double S.O.B. chases after something, because his boss is going after him. So the vicious cycle begins.

Work may be left undone because time has not been set aside for it, or because you do not know how to begin the work. The work will not be making a contribution to your department or your organization unless the work can be started. Until then, you cannot be said to have any work to do.

An idea remains an idea. The idea remains useless until you can make it happen. But you have difficulty to make it happen because you simply don't know how.

A project exists only in print if nothing is done to make things happen quickly. If the print happens to be impressively done, you may be led to think that producing the print is the project! Your project is a project only when the blue print is implemented and when tangible results are beginning to show. When you do not know how to get a project off the ground, your project is not yet a project.

Minutes of meeting run into hours without any sign of any action being taken either by you or through you by any person. At the next meeting, issues remain outstanding and at the meeting following the next, because the issues are "outstanding" they are referred to a special committee or task force for further study and discussion. Issues become outstanding because solutions remain vague. If only you had known how to get cracking to resolve the issues.

Follow-up work lapses because you have forgotten about it. That may happen once or twice, but not all the time. Perhaps you deliberately want to forget about it. So, you let your memory lapse. Perhaps you have no idea how to implement the work. Could it be that the work calls for new knowledge or new skills and you have neither? Whatever may be the true reason, the fact remains that the work that falls on you must not be left undone if you would like to keep the living terror away.

So, how do you get work done? How do you make an idea happen? How do you get a project off to a good start? How do you resolve issues? How do you execute follow-up work?

The answer lies in step #2: Observing: stated as a rule, it reads:

> "Observing is the mother of action."

A lot of things that we do are learnt through observing-looking intently at how to work things and how to make things work; how to work out plans and how to make plans work.

By observing, we are able to focus on things that matter. We are able to relate one idea to another. We are forced to reason by induction or by deduction. In the process we make decisions quicker and in a more rational way.

Let's see how this is done in practice. Supposing the task before you is to write a weekly sales report. You have never done this before.

How do you get started? You need to observe. This is done by taking out the previous sales report done by your predecessor. You then look at the way the report has been written.

How many sections are there? What are the sections called? How does each section begin? What goes into each section? You should have a fairly good idea of how a weekly sales report looks like.

Next, you need to remind yourself what you have set as the target that the weekly sales report is intended to hit as required by step #1. You need to examine critically what the report must have in order that the target can be achieved. You may have to replace some sections in the report because the sections are not helpful in achieving the target. The format of the previous report may have been designed to achieve a different purpose.

You may want to call up an ex-colleague and ask for suggestions. Will she be able to provide you with a sample? Will she be able to get one for you?

You should not rule out a trip to your favourite bookstore. If you can lay hands on an affordable book on how to write sales reports, you should do so. Alternatively, browsing through the books on display will strengthen your confidence in approaching your assigned task.

What about visiting the national public library or the libraries of the universities or polytechnics? Can you enrol as a casual or non-borrowing member? You can spend a good hour or two to take down some useful notes during the evenings or weekends.

Look out for evening courses on the topic that concerns you. These courses are intensive knowledge-imparting sessions for professionals who wish to upgrade their knowledge in various disciplines. The courses may come in different levels. Select the one with which you are most comfortable to start off. Check out with the local Chamber of Commerce, the Extra-Mural Studies Department of your local University or Polytechnic, the Community College or the Institute of Management or the Management Association.

So, remember:

> **T** o
> **O** bjectively
> **R** e-structure
> **T** asks
> **U** p front
> **R** equires
> **E** xamples.

We have seen how by observing we can get an idea on how to get started on a new activity. Can we use observing as a problem-solving tool in other areas of our work?

Let's say your job is to sell over the counter in an emporium. Your boss has asked you to increase your weekly sales target by another 50%. How do you go about achieving the new target?

Can you arrange to make a quick trip to observe how your number 1 competitor is doing? With the same product line how does your competitor draw in the crowds? How do the displays of your competitor differ from yours? How do your competitor's prices compare with yours? How fast and efficient is their wrapping service? What powerful selling tools or techniques are used by your counterpart in the competition?

The product line may not be the same in other stores, but the way sales personnel encourage shoppers and visitors to buy may give you an idea to change or modify your own approach to selling.

From observing can you suggest to your boss improvements that can be made in certain things that are not done well enough at your counter? Perhaps, there is no distinct identity of what your counter specializes in. Perhaps, you are not carrying an attractive product range or mix to make your counter a one-stop shopping point. Perhaps the counter looks drab, dismal and uninviting to shoppers. Could some piped music to improve the ambience help?

Observe which item is moving faster than the others. Observe which item is the slowest moving item. Observe who are the people who buy from you, how much they buy each time and why they buy. Find out the answers for each these questions. Make new decisions and do better things or do things in a better way.

Which item gives you the highest yield per sale? Which item gives you the lowest yield per sale? Should you not therefore put in more selling effort to increase the sale of the item which gives the highest yield per sale? Should you not therefore stock more of the more saleable item from your point of view.

Observe which day of the week and which time of the day when the traffic flow is at its peak. Are you short-handed during the peak or rush period? Can you show by having another one or two assistants to help you during the peak period, you can increase the sales substantially? Can you map out an action plan and discuss what you would like to propose with your boss?

Can you check out with course organizers whether they have a suitable course for you to attend to improve your knowledge and skills in managing retail sales? The libraries and bookstores are also places where you may be able to pick up some clever ideas to improve your work.

Step #2 also directs your attention on problem prevention. By observing what usually goes wrong, when it goes wrong, how frequently it goes wrong, why it goes wrong and what happens when it goes wrong, you can decide which problem to tackle first and how to tackle it. By observing critically you can eliminate the source of the fault whether it lies with

- The skill you are using; or

- The material you are using; or

- The machine you are using; or

- The way the task is being done; or

- The way inputs and outputs are measured at each stage of the work process.

There are two basic questions you need to ask as you apply step #2.

The first question is: "What must I be observing in order to determine whether or not the target as defined in step #1 can be achieved?"

The second question is: "What is observable that tells me 'What should be' and 'what actually is '"? The difference between what you have observed (i.e. what is) and what you have expected (i.e. what should be) will give you a positive or a negative deviation from the norm (i.e. what should be). If the deviation is negative, you will have a performance gap or a discrepancy that needs to be subsequently addressed.

STEP #3: RECORDING

"Do I know what is really happening and am I able to do something to improve the situation?"

In order to keep your Double S.O.B. further away from you, you need to implement step #3: Recording. In effect, you are moving away from expressing what you think and what you are assuming, and moving into the area where real, hard, concrete facts thrive.

Your only defence against the verbal missiles from your boss is facts; and facts are the only ammunition that can penetrate the strong fortress of your boss. You need to work with facts. Facts alone should be the basis of whatever decisions or judgments you are required to make. Without facts, you will not be able to get into his wave-length.

Step #3 is in reality a logical step that follows after step #2. Recording enables what you have observed to be kept for analysis and for further study. Recording prevents any key information from slipping away. It ensures that what you are looking for is captured and tracked all the time.

The rationale behind recording can be summed up, thus:

> **T** hrough
> **O** bjective
> **R** ecording
> **T** o
> **U** nderstand
> **R** ealities
> **E** xtensively.

To implement step #3, all you need is a couple of well-sharpened pencils and a sturdy note book. Knowing what you are looking for (step #2) is one thing; making sure that what you are looking for does not escape your attention (step #3) is another thing. Obviously, it is pointless to observe and fail to follow up what you have set out to observe without the required analysis. Analysis is impossible without sufficient relevant data being recorded. Through the right conclusions the right decisions can be made.

How do you approach the task of recording data or key information? The answer lies in the way the form is designed to capture the key data depending on the specific purpose behind what you are attempting to observe.

If you intend to find out whether or not there is a link or a relationship (i.e. a correlation) between two factors (one is known as the dependent variable and the other, the independent variable) you need to have two sets of data from two separate exercises or experiments.

For example, you may wish to establish whether or not the sales in one department (the dependent variable) are affected by the sales assistants in that department wearing high-heeled shoes (the independent variable).

You will need to conduct two experiments. The first experiment will involve sales assistants wearing flat-heeled shoes. The second experiment will involve sales assistants wearing high-heeled shoes. The duration of each experiment must be the same. Both experiments must be held outside the festive season or the sales promotion period, otherwise the results may be said to be contaminated.

You will then observe and record the actual sales generated during each period and compare the results. You will be able to conclude whether or not there is any significant difference in the sales generated because of the height of the heels of shoes worn by the sales assistants.

Let's take a look at another example. Let's say, you are responsible for answering enquiries. What do you need to record? The answer depends on what you intend to find out.

Let's say you want to install an automatic answering system to inform each enquirer to get in direct touch with the department concerned. You will therefore want to know what sort of information is usually requested. It is also useful to know when enquiries usually come in so that the department concerned can put a person on standby. The information you have recorded can also be used to develop an information booklet to be sent to enquirers.

Alternatively, you may want to develop a short training session for another person to take over your work. Recording the questions asked and what information is required will prepare the person with competence and confidence for the job.

By looking at the range of questions asked you can also obtain a fair idea of the products or types of service the public at large wants. Another inference you can draw is that certain aspects of the company's work or service are misunderstood by the public or not properly communicated to the public.

More importantly, by recording who calls, why he calls, and when he has called, you can find out later what follow-up action has been executed, whether, for example, the enquirer has got what he has asked for, or whether the enquirer has been converted into a customer for the company. That is to say, never treat any enquiry lightly. Every enquiry presents a golden selling opportunity.

Step #2 and step #3 when combined can be a very powerful tool in getting better results from your work. As an illustration, imagine you were a sales assistant in a retail outlet. Observe who the people are and who pass by your shop but who don't enter your shop. Record what you have observed. Once you know who the people are who make up the larger part of the traffic you should be able to take advantage of the situation by replacing your current sales items and merchandise by those that can zero into the tastes and interests of these people.

But, if you have already got the right merchandise and yet these people are not attracted at all, you need to observe and record other factors. Are these people rushing to and from work every day, and they need to give your shop a miss? Does your shop look unattractive? Does your shop appear to serve tourists only? Do passers-by actually know what you are selling? Why not step out of your shop, and start inviting people to visit your shop? Record how many people actually step into your shop as a result of your personal invitation. Should you not have an appropriate sign to pull in the crowds, as it is more economical and more acceptable than to have a person outside the shop to tout for business as it may be against the law?

Let's take another example. You want to know how well your competitor is doing in his business. Let's say you are in the manufacturing business. What you can do is to stand outside the factory of your competitor. Observe and record the number of trucks leaving the factory each day. Estimate how much of the merchandise is carried in each truck. You may want to observe where each truck goes in order to know who helps to distribute and sells your competitor's merchandise.

By visiting your competitor's retail outlets, and by observing and recording the price tags attached to your competitor's merchandise, you will be able to know whether your own pricing is competitive enough or not. Also by observing and recording who your competitor's customers are you will be able to re-position your products more competitively.

Another area where you can put observing and recording to effective use is in cutting down operational costs. One specific area where wastage can be effectively reduced and eventually eliminated lies in the scrap rate in your department or unit. By observing and recording what is thrown away and why it is thrown away, you will be able to do something about the situation. Without observing and recording and analyzing the cause or causes, you are literally allowing hard-earned cash being drained away day by day.

For anything that is thrown away, record what is thrown away, what its estimated cost is, and the reason why it's thrown away. The reasons for rejecting any item may be:

- Faulty material

- Unsuitable material
- Faulty equipment
- Wrong equipment
- Faulty workmanship
- Unclear instructions
- Leftovers and taking up space
- Decaying and decomposing

The preventive action you can take after analyzing the data you have observed and recorded may be:

- A more accurate specification for the supplier or change the supplier
- A machine preventive maintenance programme
- Acquiring the right equipment
- Acquiring the right knowledge and skill through formal training
- Giving clearer instructions
- Stating the quantity of output accurately
- Arranging for immediate dispatch of the food or introducing a better way of keeping it fresh.

If you are an airline stewardess, observing and recording what food items are consumed by passengers in their entirety, what items are left half-finished in the trays, and what items are generally left untouched, will help top management to make better decisions in improving in-flight meals. You are not only eliminating wastage but improving the marketing aspect of your business.

If you are a servicing technician, both steps #2 and #3 can help you to locate the part of the machine which tends to cause breakdowns, or identify the sub-system which needs special attention periodically, or determine the spare parts that are in frequent demand. The data you have recorded will help you to do an analysis and help you to make the right suggestions which you can submit to the design engineer or the supplier.

If you are a library assistant, you may want to observe and record what books are never left on the shelves for longer than one day, two days or three days. On the other hand, it would be useful to know what books other than reference books remain unborrowed, or seldom borrowed. Library space is expensive and what you want to make sure is that the space is not wasted, so that the wrong books that are in the library should be replaced by more books of the kind that appeal most to the library members and visitors. You may also want to observe and record the number of books borrowed. If the number of books borrowed is expressed as a percentage of the total number of books the library has, you will have a fair idea of whether or not your books suit the needs of your library members.

Another important area where you can reduce operational costs is by observing and recording where your time in the organization goes. Could it be that you are spending 80% of your time on low value activities, and only 20% of your time on activities that have a high payoff? It is when you don't get your 80-20 ratio right that you feel disillusioned.

So start observing and recording what you do each day. How long is each activity? Does it carry a low, medium or high value in terms of contributing to your role and the daily or weekly or monthly targets that you need to hit? Does the activity involve other people, meeting people, talking to people or travelling most of the time?

Once you have got the data recorded you can analyze where your time goes. You can then re-arrange your work pattern in such a way that if you need to meet external clients you can schedule to meet them on the same day. You can put aside an hour, for example, to make return calls, so that each time when somebody calls on you, you can tell the caller you will give him a return call. In this way, you can reduce to some extent the disruption to your work caused by the telephone.

Do you spend enough time checking out work contracted to others, like suppliers and external sub-contractors? Do you spend enough time discussing with the clients and customers and clarifying what their expectations are?

Each time as you pick up a task to do, it is helpful to remind yourself by asking whether or not by what you are doing, it will contribute to making a better product or providing a better service for the customers. Anything done not towards this end must be viewed with suspicion.

STEP #4: TRACKING

"Do I have a system in place to keep things under real control?"

The next step helps you to keep your focus in place. It enables you to follow through from making sure you have set a target to checking whether or not the target has been achieved. It ensures that there is no intermediate break in the chain of activities or tasks that must be done correctly.

Step #4: tracking, as it is called, essentially requires you to do two things. The first is to think through all the things that must be planned in advance and organized in order that a particular target can be achieved. The second is to make sure that each of the things to be done is actually done and done properly, and if there is anything to be done by another person, to make sure that that person has done it and done it properly.

What tracking can do is to achieve the following:

- There is consistency of purpose directed at a specific target;

- There is a prompt transformation whereby an input becomes an output;

- There is a series of control and check points to monitor progress;

- There is no breakdown in the chain of tasks to be executed; and

- There is immediate knowledge of the status of the object that enters the system.

In the course of carrying out an activity anything can happen to disrupt or frustrate the smooth completion of the activity.

If you are a motorist driving along an express way what may or can happen which may cause an accident? Your car may skid because of heavy oil patches along the bend, or coming out of a bend right in front of you in the inner lane is a stationary truck. Or in the middle of the night you have an elderly man walking across the road, or if you are in the countryside a cow may dash out in front of you. The brakes of your car may fail. A car from the other side of the road may be overtaking another car and suddenly appears in front of you. You may be hit by a flying object; where it comes, you have no idea. In each of these circumstances what would you do?

Tracking means when an important object enters an activity or work or production process you are able to trace the route the object takes and to do something in time before the object gets into any form of trouble. So in the case of the motorist, the activity (or in the language of the organization, work process) is driving from point X to point Y, the object entering the activity is the car (together with the driver and the other occupants in the car). Tracking ensures that the car will have a safe journey along the route until it arrives at its destination (i.e. the target of the activity).

Let's take another example. A person calls up your organization. He wants to know what type of service your company is offering. Here the activity or work process is receiving an enquiry and converting it into a sale. The object entering the work process is an enquiry.

Tracking as applied to handling an enquiry would mean that you make sure that the enquiry is not lost or left unattended to as it enters the organization and that as it emerges from the organization it becomes an instruction to you to place an order. The enquiry (an input) has become a sale (an output) as a result of the value-adding process. Anything that comes to you should not leave you without more value added to it.

Let's look at another example. A person enters your store, a large emporium operating in a well-known plaza in the city. She may not have any thing in mind to buy. She is simply a window-shopper. The question you need to ask is: Does my company have a system whereby every window-shopper that enters the store is carefully looked after so that when she leaves the store she will emerge as a cheerful, satisfied customer? Or do you leave all visitors to your store to wander about, enjoy the music and the cool air, and be amazed at the range of new merchandise you display and eventually leave your store empty-handed? Without putting in place step #4: tracking, this will be the scenario that you are getting.

As a powerful tool in helping you to align your work towards organizational excellence, and in so doing, keeping your Double S.O.B. further away from you, do remember that:

> **T** racking
> **O** ptimizes
> **R** esources;
> **T** racking
> **U** ndisputably
> **R** einforces
> **E** xcellence.

How do you actually set up a tracking system? The primary function of the system is to prevent any object, task or activity that is passed to you from getting lost and to ensure that when the object, task or activity leaves you, it has acquired more value. To be able to fulfill this function the system must be able to do the following things:

- Record the day and the time of receipt;

- Pinpoint the day and the time of the critical action to be followed up;

- List the step-by-step tasks leading to the achievement of the target;

- List the likely disruptions that may intervene; and

- List the counter or preventive measures that may be required.

In effect, you need to do a number of things which are:

- Writing down the target you intend to achieve as required in step #1 ;

- Observing and writing down what must be done by you to achieve the target as required in step #2 and step #3;

- Observing and recording what may possibly go wrong and what may be done to prevent any mishap from occurring as part of the tracking exercise in step #4; and

- Writing down what should be done to avert an accident should adverse conditions occur as part of the tracking exercise in step #4.

Let's see how you can put tracking into practice. For instance, a customer wants to send his car for regular servicing. Your first task is to note the time the car is delivered to you. Since regular servicing requires routine work the time taken is known. You then look at the number of outstanding jobs already lined up. You can then estimate when the car is ready for collection. To add in a safety margin you give a 10% allowance for any unexpected delay. You will then enter in the log the expected time of collection. Your next task is to tell the customer when to collect the car.

A number of things can happen. The car may need special attention and you need to communicate this to the customer. Or the job may be delayed because of unforeseen circumstances and again you need to let the customer know. So, you need to know how to contact the customer during the time the car is in your care. The customer's telephone number and contact address are also entered in your log. There should be a checklist of tasks to be done, and in what sequence, and by whom, and how long each task takes for cars requiring routine check-up and servicing. From your log, you should be able to tell at what time the car should be going through what stage of the process. You can also call up the individual technician or engineer to confirm if you need to do so.

A number of things may happen to the car. Scratches, smudges and traces of paint may be left on the car. Things inside the car may be gone over or removed. The car may catch fire. The car may be stolen. Thus, you need to come up with procedures on how to handle the car and who should handle the procedures.

As an added precaution, if everything that can be possibly done by you and your colleagues to prevent any damage or loss to the car is actually done, and yet a mishap occurs, have you taken out an insurance policy to cover risks outside your control?

Tracking requires you to think through and to list what can possibly happen to the object and/or activity passed to you for attention. In our example, the object is the customer's car and the activity is regular servicing. You want to know what must be done to prevent things from going wrong. You must be able to tell what is happening to the object and/or the activity. You must be able to know what the most critical follow-up action is and which is planned to happen and when. In our example the critical follow-up action is calling up the customer to tell him that his car is ready for collection.

Can you state the object and/or the activity to be tracked from the list below? What are the main components of each tracking system?

- A customer wishes to open a current account with your bank.

- A customer complains that she has been wrongly billed.

- A customer sends a coat to be dry-cleaned.

- A mother delivers her two-year old baby to your day nursery.

- You run a two-hour training session for children wanting to learn tennis.

STEP #5: UNRAVELLING

"Do I really know how to locate and solve problems?"

How you solve problems and how fast you can solve problems are not the only two questions that you must answer every day. You need to know also how competent and speedy you are in locating problems. If you want to keep your boss another hundred meters away from you, you need to acquire the art and technique that will help you to:

- Locate and pinpoint accurately where the problem is;

- State precisely and concisely the cause of the problem; and

- Act swiftly to remove the cause of the problem.

You must always do these three things before your boss comes to know that there is a problem. Whether or not you have already started to work on the problem is besides the point. Once your Double S.O.B. knows that there is a problem, to him, you have become a problem! So you must resolve problems before they get to his knowledge.

Step #5: unravelling will show you how to apply the right approach to locating and solving problems within your own work area.

The word "problem" is itself problematic. It can mean different things to different people. Each meaning is taken from the angle or perspective the user has adopted. When we do not see eye to eye on the same thing and yet we think we do, we are unlikely to improve the situation. Unless the real issue in question is resolved, the problem will remain as a problem, although we may have swept it under the carpet.

It is common to hear people complaining of having to go through life with financial or family problems, of having to work every day with problem employees, of having to sleep with work-related problems, of having to resolve the problem of finding more time for their work, or having to cope with the problem of meeting deadlines all the time.

Where do we actually start in order to end all these problems? Can we actually solve them, or are they here to stay? The starting point is the way we define a problem. Nine chances out of ten will find us unable to solve a problem because our focus or direction is led away from the real solution. We begin to tackle issues that do not actually help us to remove the problem. We may even make the problem become worse, such as when a mother without the right medical knowledge attempts to treat her child suffering from burns.

So before you proceed, in the space below, write down what you think a problem is:

A problem is _____
_____
_____

How did you define or describe a problem? Imagine you have been delivered 1,000 units of an item on 1st June. Up to today, 31st July, you have still got 800 units in your inventory. Today is the last day when the entire lot is expected to be sold. What is your problem? Is your problem . . . .?

- ...... how to clear the remaining stock within a week without incurring a loss?

- ...... where to find additional space for a batch of new items that will be delivered in the next seven days?

- ...... why you have ordered in excess of what you can sell?

- ...... how to explain to your boss why the item is moving at such a slow pace?

- ...... how to decide which is the real problem?

Most of the time we may not be attacking the real problem but managing the effect or consequence of the problem. When we cannot remove or mitigate the effect of the first problem, a new problem has emerged. If we don't attack the cause of the first problem, it may happen again and again.

In the example above which is the first or original problem which if not solved will happen again? Which problem is related to managing the damage done by the first problem? When you cannot manage the consequence satisfactorily with the minimum of loss possible, what is the next problem that will occur in the chain?

Thus, you can see that when something goes wrong in the organization, very often it will create a chain of events and reactions and you will be faced with more than one problem, not forgetting that facing your boss is a problem itself!

So, what is a problem?

As a working definition, a problem may be defined as any unexpected gap caused by an intervening event (or events) so that the original target or intention becomes unattainable.

For example, you intend to sell 1,000 units of an item in two months' time between 1st June and 31st July. This has been set as your target. But by 31st July, only 200 units have been sold. The gap which is the 800 units that remain to be sold is the problem.

In the next seven days you need space for a new shipment of goods. But if space is unavailable, when the goods arrive you will have a problem. Your boss expects you to be able to solve problems. That is why he figures he needs you. So, you cannot pass him the two problems you are now facing.

Since your boss is going to be very rough with you, how can you solve both problems in time before he knows about the problems? If you can achieve that, you have got yourself out of a third problem, your Double S.O.B. You may say that you would not have any problem had you not had a Double S.O.B. He was the one who placed the order for 1,000 units in the first place, without consulting anyone in the organization!

Even if that being the case, whenever you find you cannot achieve the original target, you need to swing into immediate action to manage the consequence caused by the shortfall. In our example, the consequence that is to be managed is the question of space. You may want to check whether the new shipment can be delayed without creating new problems. Or do you still have time to sell the remaining inventory? What must you do so that in the end the new shipment is not affected and you can reduce any likely loss to the organization to the minimum?

Only after you have done what you must do urgently then should you direct your mind to investigating why in the first place the problem has happened. What you do next is prevention so that the same problem will not occur again.

As a further illustration. A customer has come to you to complain that her new hair dryer has a faulty mechanism. Finding out why the product cannot be defects-free should not be your immediate attention. Here you have an angry or dissatisfied customer. If you don't manage the situation well enough you will create a second problem. She will not come back to your shop again; besides, she is going to tell her friends about her experience, and you are going to lose valuable business from her network of potential customers. You must do something to make a quick service recovery, so that she can go away, reassured that she can get value from her purchase.

What you do, after she has gone away, to make sure that all other hair dryers of the same brand and model do not have the same fault then becomes important and urgent. You will follow up with a report to the production manager so that the future batch of hair dryers coming off the assembly line can be 100% free of defects.

How do we tackle a problem, once we know that there is a problem? But, do we actually know what the problem is? There is no point working on something about which you have only a vague idea. You should be able to state in not more than twelve words, what the problem is precisely, and where precisely the problem is located. Once you have done that, the next thing you must do is to investigate in order to determine the main cause of the problem.

The two sides of the problem coin are the effect and the cause(s). As pointed out earlier, we address the effect first before tackling the causes(s). If the effect is not addressed, there may be additional problems to solve.

So, the effect of unsold inventory is the unavailability of space for the new shipment and the inability to hit the sales target. If the new shipment is delayed because of the space problem another unfavorable situation is created. In the example of the faulty hair dryer, the effect is an angry customer. Here again, if the angry customer goes away still being angry, the resulting effect may be a nasty letter to your company's chairman and loss of potential business when the angry customer spreads the word around.

The problem we have before us is the gap that separates the <u>targeted situation </u>(as indicated in the target to be achieved) and the<u> actual situation</u> (as indicated in the actual achievement). What has happened as an intervening factor or event is the major cause of the gap.

Let's say the item for which you have an excess or surplus of 800 units is made up of sun-glasses for ladies.

From previous experience you know that June and July are hot months and ladies buy sun-glasses before heading for the beach. That has been the trend, say for the past three to four years, and that's the reason for placing the huge order of 1,000 units.

You have expected the supply would be taken up very quickly with orders coming from optical shops, supermarkets and department stores. But the fact remains that orders have come from only 8% of the targeted retailers, and each order was for only five to ten units. Could it be that:

- June and July have become exceptionally wet?

- There has been an upsurge of interest for vacations in countries abroad with cool weathers?

- Spread of fear that sun-glasses are harmful to the eyes?

- Sun-glasses are no longer in fashion?

- Retailers have ceased to promote sun-glasses?

- Consumers are tightening their belts because of an impending recession?

- Ladies have switched to indoor activities?

- Ladies give up the beach in preference for the air-conditioned cinema?

- Retailers have a higher profit margin promoting and selling other items for the executive fashion-conscious ladies?

- Your competitors have come out with new brands of sun-glasses?

- Sun-glasses with earphones to receive radio broadcasts are in vogue?

- Your sun-glasses are overpriced?

- Your sun-glasses are unattractive?

- Your sun-glasses are defective?

- Your sun-glasses do not have non-refractive lenses?

- Your sun-glasses do not come with an attractive, protective, compact case?

- Your sun-glasses come only in one style and size?

- Your sun-glasses are not designed to match ladies outdoor wear?

- Your sales and marketing personnel have not done what they should have done as in previous years?

- Top management has not helped in monitoring and managing the sales?

There can be many likely causes why those retail outlets as targeted in your plan have not placed for orders as expected.

The sixty-four-thousand-dollar question that still remains is: "What has caused the sale to drop from the expected 1,000 units to 200?"

Perhaps, was there an antecedent problem, one that came before the present one? What might that be?

Could it be that the one who placed the order for the 1,000 units of ladies' sun-glasses had a problem in coming to the right decision? The problem would be that he had over-estimated the number sold by 80%.

What could be the main cause? Could it be that he ....?

- .....did not know how to work out a sales forecast?

- ......did not do what he ought to do to be able to make an accurate sales forecast?

- .....did not know on what the sales targets of the previous years were based?

- ......did not check the basis of the sales projections submitted by retail outlets that were surveyed?

- ......did not choose the right companies for the survey?

- ....did not ask the right question?

- ......did not get the retail outlets to place orders for a specific quantity?

- ......did not get new retail outlets to place a trial order?

- ......did not arrange for delivery to be executed in stages spread over a longer time scale?

- ....did not work out a plan to secure new markets?

How will you know which cause was chiefly responsible for the inability to make the right decision which would have been to place an order for 200 units of ladies' sun-glasses?

Once you know what the problem is, how do you find out what the main cause of the problem is?

What you need to do is to list the things that were done and check whether or not each of those things was done correctly.

If after checking what should have been done, and whether they had been done correctly, then you should list a few things which were not done and check whether or not the problem could have been prevented if any of those things should have been done and whether they had been done correctly.

Something done wrongly so as to cause something unwanted to happen can be the cause of the problem.

For example, if you should be checking whether companies were interested in what you intended to sell, and you had gone around to check, but if it happened that you had checked the wrong retail outlets, then the answers you had obtained would have become counter-productive and not only irrelevant. The answers would then constitute the unwanted thing, and they could become the main cause of your problem.

Alternatively, something not done when it should be done may cause an unwanted thing to happen and this can be the cause of the problem, too.

For example, if you should be checking whether your competitors would be bringing out a new product to compete with yours, and you had not done that, it would result in your ignorance of not knowing what was actually going on at the marketplace. This ignorance would become the unwanted thing and it would become the cause of your problem.

Let's take a closer look at the problem-solving approach in a diagrammatic form as shown below:

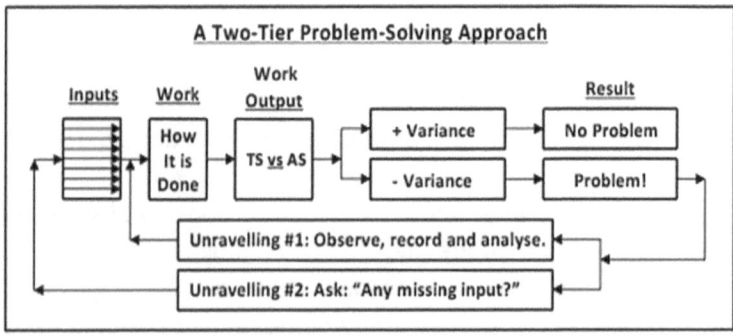

Unravelling #1: Observe, Record and Analyse

The fundamental question that needs to be answered is: "What has gone wrong in what has been done?"

To answer that **question** you need to carry out three tasks: observe, record and analyse.

Things you need to observe are:

- All the inputs coming into the work process, e.g. materials, machines, information, etc.;

- All the tasks that are executed, what each task is about, and how each task is carried out;

- The conditions that exist when each task is executed.

Things you need to record are:

- The characteristics that make up the 'quality" of each input;

- The performance standard or result of each task that has been executed;

- The conditions that exist when each task is being executed.

Things you need to analyse are:

- Determining whether the actual "quality" of each input matches its expected "quality";

- Determining whether the result or the performance standard of each task conforms to the expected result or standard;

- Determining whether there is any change in the conditions when each task is being executed;

- Detecting whether there is any causal link between one factor (e.g. institutional customers) and another factor (e.g. time taken for invoices to be settled).

Unravelling #2: Ask: "Any missing input?"

The fundamental question that needs to be answered is: "Is there anything that needs to be done but has not been done and yet it is essential in order to arrive eventually at the targeted situation?"

To answer that question you need to carry out three tasks: reflect, hypothesize and test.

In reflecting, you need to:

- Go through the entire work process mentally and ask whether anything has been missed out;

- Enrich your thinking process by talking with people whom you know can help to enlighten you or by reading books or journals related to the work you are doing, or by observing how your competitors do.

In hypothesizing, you need to:

- List the likely causes of the problem;

- Cross out, through the process of elimination, those causes that are less likely to have caused the problem.

In testing, you need to:

- Put the hypothesis to the test, by actually carrying out the experiment;

- Observe, record and analyse as you would in carrying out unravelling in step #1.

By using unravelling #1 and #2, you should be able to introduce either corrective actions or preventive measures to reduce or eliminate wastage, rejects, and customer complaints. In effect you have less stress to carry as the acronym below says:

> **T** rouble
> **O** vercome
> **R** eleases
> **T** ension
> **U** nless
> **R** e-work
> **E** merges.

STEP #6: RE-DEFINING

"Do I take a step back to review and reflect on my work, relate it to corporate objectives and re-focus, re-structure and refine what I should do?"

The next step in the T.O.R.T.U.R.E. process that will continue to increase the distance, physically and emotionally, between you and your Double S.O.B. is one which helps you to:

- Take stock of what you have been doing;

- Reflect on what and how you should do better the next time around;

- Relate one variable to another variable;

- Re-focus, re-structure and refine work to increase the certainty of its completion and its impact;

- Get each task reviewed and re-vamped to prevent problems from arising;

- Be more conscious of the vital need to build customer loyalty.

The 6 R's that make up yet another important step in helping you to step out of the shadow of your Double S.O.B. are reading, reflecting, relating, re-focusing, re-structuring and refining. They rely heavily on your ability to think through things supported by the other abilities: target-setting, observing, recording, tracking and unravelling, which we have already touched upon in the previous sections.

The way we define what we want to achieve (targets), or how we do a task (the methodology), or what we want to solve (problems) is the key to our success in our work. If our starting point is wrong, if our aim is imprecise, if our target is vague, no matter what we do we cannot put our objectives right.

Having defined something we need to re-define it to get it 100 percent right. Defining it the first time may not hit the bull's eye, but re-defining it may.

As an example, if you define one of your personal problems as having insufficient time to pursue a part-time degree course, you will never be taking up such a course. Why? Simple. Because the way you define your responsibility moves you away from what you can do. Putting the blame on not having enough time reassures yourself that you are not to blame, time is!

Everybody has the same amount of time. Nobody is having more or less than what another person has. We are all given 86,400 units of time (measured in seconds) every day. Different people use what they are given in different ways with different pay-offs. Whether or not you would like to take, say 7,200 units out of each day for your intellectual pursuit is entirely up to you: not up to Time. If you prefer to spend the 7,200 units in watching the television or in window-shopping, you cannot say that you don't have enough time to study.

So, the problem is not finding time, nor is it scheduling time. The problem may lie in your inability to see yourself getting a degree important and urgent enough to want to set aside a certain amount of time each day to help you achieve your goal say, in five years' time.

How we define an issue or problem is how we are going to approach and tackle the issue or problem. We may define it, like the example above, in such a way that prevents us from examining the real cause and from taking the right action.

The definition you give to a phenomenon or an issue may well restrict your thinking and your creativity unnecessarily. So, your targets must be defined and re-defined to a point where they are precise, relevant and attainable.

In order to achieve the 6 R's as shown in the diagram below, you need to examine each "R" in turn:

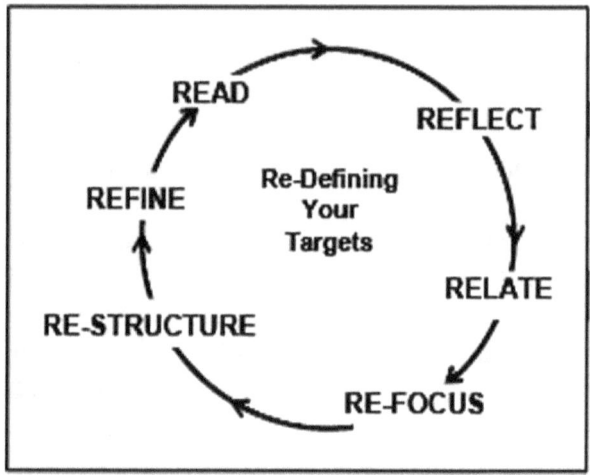

Reading

Do you read to get ahead in your career or do you read just for pleasure? If you say you have no time to read professionally, you should not be reading just because you think you can make life worth living by doing that!

Do you therefore read selectively and perceptively? Do you read with an open mind? Do you read to analyze what you have noted or recorded from what you have observed or measured?

Do you proofread everything carefully and accurately before sending out what you have vetted, approved or signed?

Do you read with the occasional jotting down of key points for recall, important ideas for further study and useful things you can and should do at work?

Read extensively and intensively and you will see how reading can help you re-define your goals, your values and your career aspirations.

Reflecting

Do you always make it a point to go over mentally how you have executed a task and what you can learn from it or how you should approach a new task?

Do you just dismiss that "luck" was not with you when things didn't turn out the way they should have turned out? Or do you think over critically what could have gone wrong?

Before you doze off each night, do you think over a problem or a new situation you are going to encounter the next day?

By reflecting you will be able to re-define the way things ought to be done to produce not different or faster results but better results.

Relating

Do you continuously seek to establish the relationship between one thing and another or between one set of data and another set of data?

Do you set out to verify whether there is any causal link or relationship between a given variable (e.g. wages) and a work-related phenomenon (e.g. employee turnover)?

Do you always make a conscious effort to relate the technical features of a product to the specific needs of your customers or clients, thereby turning technical features into saleable benefits?

By relating apparently unrelated things you will be able to re-define the likely outcome of a new phenomenon or a new interaction of factors.

Re-focusing

Do you always take your bearings from a new perspective? Are you sensitive to the changes in the business environment? Are you alert to what your competitors are doing or will be doing to take away your share of the market?

Do you always check to see whether any work you do has outlived its original purpose and therefore ought to be re-focused to fulfil a new purpose?

Do you keep looking at old things with increasing curiosity and excitement as new ideas and challenges never cease to emerge?

Do you not shift your attention from one goal to another, but tackle constantly the same goal with greater intensity and persistence until successful completion?

By re-focusing your work, you can re-define your role in as well as your contributions to the enterprise.

Re-structuring

How can your work be re-structured to make its flow less erratic and problematic?

How can your department or the unit under your charge be re-structured so that the current informal reporting channels can be legitimized?

Can you take a given task and break it down into steps and re-sequence the steps in a way to eliminate any bottlenecks that may slow down the completion of the task?

By re-structuring work you can re-define the completion time for any given task or activity as well as re-setting the performance standards that need to be achieved.

Refining

The key word here is "better". There is no point refining or perfecting what you do, unless it results in a better product or a better service for your clients and customers.

Hence, your targets will undergo the re-defining process, to ensure that all targets will trigger work in the organization aimed at building customer loyalty.

Seriously you should be questioning whether what you do is in fact contributing towards making a better and better product for customers or towards providing a better and better service day by day.

Refining work has the effect of making each event, or task, or activity failure-proof. Before putting a new service or a new product in the market, you need to test the service procedure or field-test the prototype.

When you are certain that each task or step is capable of being executed 100% right all the time, you have refined your work to a point where problems can be effectively prevented.

Thus, by re-defining what you should be achieving in terms of your role, your work and your contributions in producing products or supplying a service that people are willing to buy, there is one golden rule that you need to remember, and that is:

> **T** hrough
> **O** bjective
> **R** e-defining,
> **T** argets
> **U** ndergo
> **R** ealistic
> **E** xamination.

STEP #7: EXPEDITING

"Do I really know how the time taken up by each work process is distributed?"

We now come to the final step in the T.O.R.T.U.R.E. process, another important step that will keep your Double S.O.B. at a safe distance.

Expediting, as it is called, requires you to do two things: first of all to be time-conscious, to ask always whether something can be done by half the time it would normally take to be completed. You need to bear in mind that a decision if not executed quickly, can be overtaken by new events. If you don't bring out your product fast enough, you become not a market leader but a copycat. The effect of what you do may become irrelevant if there is a delay because the circumstances may have changed in the meantime.

Secondly, you need to be opportunity-conscious, to ask always whether you can see something happening or not happening so that you can do something to your favour, or even turn an adversity or a very bad situation around to your favour.

Expediting does not deal with the speed of work or the pace of an activity only, although how quickly you do something is important.

Expediting primarily deals with how quickly you can start doing the so-called first task. If you decide to wall-paper your living room, your first task might be going down to the emporium to get a roll of wallpaper, or peeling off the existing wall paper.

If you have to write a report, what might be your first task? It might be to get a copy of the previous report to serve as a model. Or, it might be writing down the outline of your report. Or, it might be defining the purpose of the report after determining who will read the report and why.

Expediting also essentially means getting a number of first tasks of different activities or projects to start at the same time or almost in parallel, followed by other tasks.

A helpful technique that you can use is the matrix chart as shown below:

Date/Time					
Project	T	A	S	K	S
"A"					
"B"					
"C"					
"D"					

Executive Tasks Running in Parallel

If it is humanly impossible for you to do a couple of things at the same or about the same time, can you farm out what you have to do?

Expediting requires you to map out the entire work process and to use a stop-watch to time how long each stage or step or task takes to be completed.

You need to be critical and therefore inquisitive about the length of time each stage takes to be completed.

For example, how long does it take for a letter to be replied? Once the letter is deposited at the counter by the postman what happens to the letter? How long does it take before the addressee actually reads the letter? How long before the addressee drafts the reply? Must the draft reply be sent to another person for vetting? To whom is the draft reply sent for typing? How long does it take the draft to reach the typist? How long does the draft reply remain with the typist before the type-written reply emerges? How long does it take for the reply to reach the post office? What is the total cycle time?

How much time is wasted while the letter or the input is lying idle for something to be done to it, i.e. waiting time?

How much time is taken up moving the letter or the output from one place to another, i.e. transporting time?

How much time is required in adding value to each input, i.e. production time?

How much time is spent in executing corrective action or re-doing the work i.e. re-work time?

Waiting time, transporting time and re-work time are actually wasted time. They need to be eliminated or reduced.

The form as shown below can capture the needed data to enable you to calculate the total cycle time. You can also calculate the percentage of time that is wasted and do something about it.

	TRIGGER	STAGE	STAGE	STAGE	Finished Product	Delivery	Total
Waiting Time							
Transporting Time							
Production Time							
Re-work Time							
						Total Cycle Time	

Calculating the Total Cycle Time for Each Activity

By recording what is actually happening and subsequently analyzing the data, you may be able to draw inferences that will enable you to:

- Cut down time that is wasted;

- Reduce production time;

- Re-structure the tasks;

- Re-sequence the order of tasks;

- Re-arrange the tasks to run in parallel;

- Replace existing tasks by new tasks; or

- Replace existing procedures by new procedures.

In planning a new activity, you need to do reverse thinking. You need to work backwards from the expected date and time of delivery of output to the first task.

Let's say you are required to deliver to your client a made-to-measure jacket on the 15th August. Today is the 12th August. Are you sure you can deliver the jacket within three days?

You need to list all the tasks required such as getting the exact measurements, drawing out the pattern, purchasing the material, cutting, patching, fitting, sewing, putting on the buttons, ironing, packing and delivering. For each task, you need to estimate the time that it will take to be completed.

What is the total cycle time? You need to allow time for waiting, transporting and re-doing. If the total cycle time falls outside the three-day period, you need to eliminate wasted time and also to shorten production time. If the total cycle time is, say three hours only, when must the first task start at the latest?

The organizational resource that is truly unique is time. Unlike money, or any other resource, time cannot be borrowed, leased or stored. It must be spent and spent in a way that makes it more of an investment and less of a cost or an expenditure.

Investment time refers to time spent in making the company's products better and better or in keeping the company's service always ahead of your competitors in the business.

Expenditure time refers to time spent in keeping things going, in restoring the status quo and in preventing the business from slowing down. It does not deal with business growth as does investment time.

Expediting will help you to enlarge your investment time at the expense of your expenditure time. In effect, you will be doing more planning with proper target-setting to provide the requisite direction. You will be tracking each task by observing, recording and analyzing data to monitor its progress through the production process.

Through unravelling problems and issues you will be taking either corrective action or implementing preventive measures to eliminate defective products and breakdowns in customer service.

The rationale behind getting better products out quicker and providing faster, superior customer service is found in the final acronym as follows:

T imeliness
O ptimizes
R eturn;
T ime
U nchecked
R educes
E fficiency.

CONCLUSION

T.O.R.T.U.R.E.

ARE YOU YOURSELF A BOSS?

TAKING STOCK OF WHAT YOU HAVE ACHIEVED

You will have learnt ways to....

- Reduce the time spent in planning your work and working your plans now that you have the T.O.R.T.U.R.E. system to guide you.

- Feel more in control over your own work as you are able to set meaningful and measurable targets now that you are able to track and evaluate work within the context of your role and responsibilities.

- Deal with your 'burnout' feelings that will not destroy your career but develop it.

- Develop a positive frame of mind, ever ready to deal with any situation involving your boss in an assertive, professional way.

- Get things moving in the right direction, in the right way within your own area of work and accountability.

The important question now is, if you have subordinates who report directly to you, how do you think they view your authority figure?

Will they see you as the First Among Equals or as a Double S.O.B.?

Will you be able to provide a supportive, nurturing, conflict-free climate that encourages the best to come out from each person?

Will you be able to lead, but not manage, them? Are you sincere enough to want to develop the potential of each one, and to reward each justly and equitably according to each person's performance?

SELF-PERCEPTION CHECK QUIZ

Give yourself the following quiz to see how you think your subordinates will rate you as their immediate supervisor. Put a tick () in the appropriate column for each of the ten questions below:

	NO	NOT SURE	YES
1. Do you lead by setting the right examples?			
2. Do you set clear, achievable targets?			
3. Do you write plainly and clearly in all your instructions?			
4. Do you provide sufficient resources for each new assignment?			
5. Do you always focus on what the person does and not on the person?			
6. Do you advise, guide and coach with patience and enthusiasm?			
7. Do you exercise patience, forbearance and understanding when mistakes occur?			
8. Do you reward every one fairly and generously?			
9. Do you encourage the other person to recommend solutions and suspend your own?			
10. Do you always listen, encourage the other person to talk, clarify what you hear, conclude what you have heard, and check and test your conclusions in that order?			
Total			

VERDICT: ARE YOU A FIRST AMONG EQUALS

Scoring:

Add up the number of responses in each column. A "no" response earns -1 point. A "yes" response earns +1 point. A "not sure" response earns no point. Calculate your aggregate score.

Circle the numeral below that corresponds to your aggregate score:

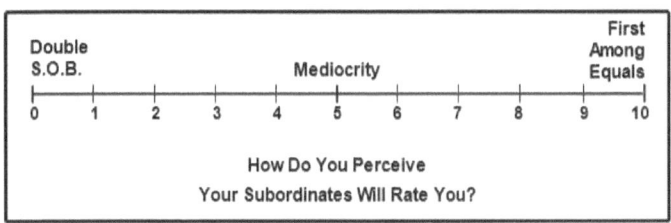

If your score is above 7.5 you regard yourself to be perceived by others as the First Among Equals.

If your score is below 4.5, you perceive others will rate you as one tending towards the Double S.O.B.!

A score that is between 4.5 and 7.5 means that you see yourself as possessing average leadership qualities.

How different do you think your perception is when compared with the way your subordinates will rate you? To answer that, you should actually give your subordinates each the quiz and see what the average score is like.

May the average score turn out to be above 7.5!

Good luck.

About the Author

Jimmy Low brings twelve years of studies of "bosses" to the development of this unique system-*cum*-guide that provides proven tactics and techniques to manage one's immediate superior, no matter how nasty and mean s/he is. He has been active in interpersonal relations diagnosis and development projects for large organizations in both the private and public sectors in the Asia Pacific region.

In his varied roles at different times in the past twenty years as Management Development Manager, Management Educator, Training Manager, Management Consultant, and HRD Director, he has worked with a wide range of "bosses" and "leaders" from public utilities, airlines, educational institutions, and service industries.

When it comes to the realities of political strife in the corporate world, Jimmy has had first-hand experience of what it is like to have a boss who is not a leader and to have a leader who is not a boss. *Hence*, the practical bias which the book has adopted.

Jimmy is a frequent speaker at management workshops and seminars on topics and themes which include Managing One's Boss and Managing Difficult Subordinates. He is the author of several books including "Managing Difficult Subordinates", "Winning Tactics for Managers", "I.M.P.A.C.T. Strategy" and "An Integrated Approach to HRM".

Among his academic credentials, the one that has the closest link to this book is his M.Sc. Degree in Industrial Relations.

www.ingramcontent.com/pod-product-compliance
Lightning Source LLC
Chambersburg PA
CBHW030838180526
45163CB00004B/1375